A–Z OF DEVIZES

PLACES - PEOPLE - HISTORY

Michael Burgess

AMBERLEY

First published 2026

Amberley Publishing
The Hill, Stroud, Gloucestershire, GL5 4EP
www.amberley-books.com

ISBN 978 1 3981 2973 3 (print)
ISBN 978 1 3981 2974 0 (ebook)

British Library Cataloguing in Publication Data.
A catalogue record for this book is available from the British Library.

Typesetting by SJmagic DESIGN SERVICES, India.
Printed in Great Britain.

Appointed GPSR EU Representative: Easy Access System Europe Oü, 16879218
Address: Mustamäe tee 50, 10621, Tallinn, Estonia
Contact Details: gpsr.requests@easproject.com, +358 40 500 3575

Contents

Introduction

Devizes is a market town in the centre of Wiltshire on the very edge of the Vale of Pewsey. It grew up around a Norman castle, although some speculate that it was founded by King Dunwallo, who ruled before the arrival of the Romans.

Over the centuries, it has been besieged twice. After the castle was destroyed by the Parliamentarians under Oliver Cromwell, Devizes grew in prosperity, becoming famous for cloth weaving, holding the largest corn market in the west of England and later for the brewing of beer.

Remarkably for such a small town, Devizes has no fewer than 500 listed buildings. It is also home to four Church of England churches as well as places of worship for many other faiths.

To the west of the town centre lies Caen Hill Locks, the tall flight of twenty-nine locks on the Kennet and Avon Canal. Built in 1810, it is one of the longest continuous flights of locks in England. There are nineteen in the steepest portion approaching the town and leading to Devizes Wharf.

I hope this book will allow you to explore the history and architecture of Devizes from a new perspective. As ever in any book of this length, I have had to be selective in my choices of things and places to cover, and I apologise if I have missed out any of your favourites.

A

Albion Place

Hidden just around the corner from Devizes High Street, Albion Place is the home of local music and artistic shops and the *Devizes Pyramid* (of which more later). A statue of James Dean stares down thoughtfully from the veranda at the passing world.

Built in the early nineteenth century, Albion Place is officially part of Sidmouth Street. It is made up of two adjoining symmetrical houses, connected by a full-width veranda above three arches with square columns, all under a slate roof.

Cositas Bonitas offer a wide range of hand-made artistic gifts, while the Light and Sounds music shop are happy to provide you with any instruments you might require. All this while happily restringing your guitar, as they have done since 1993.

Albion Place on Sidmouth Street.

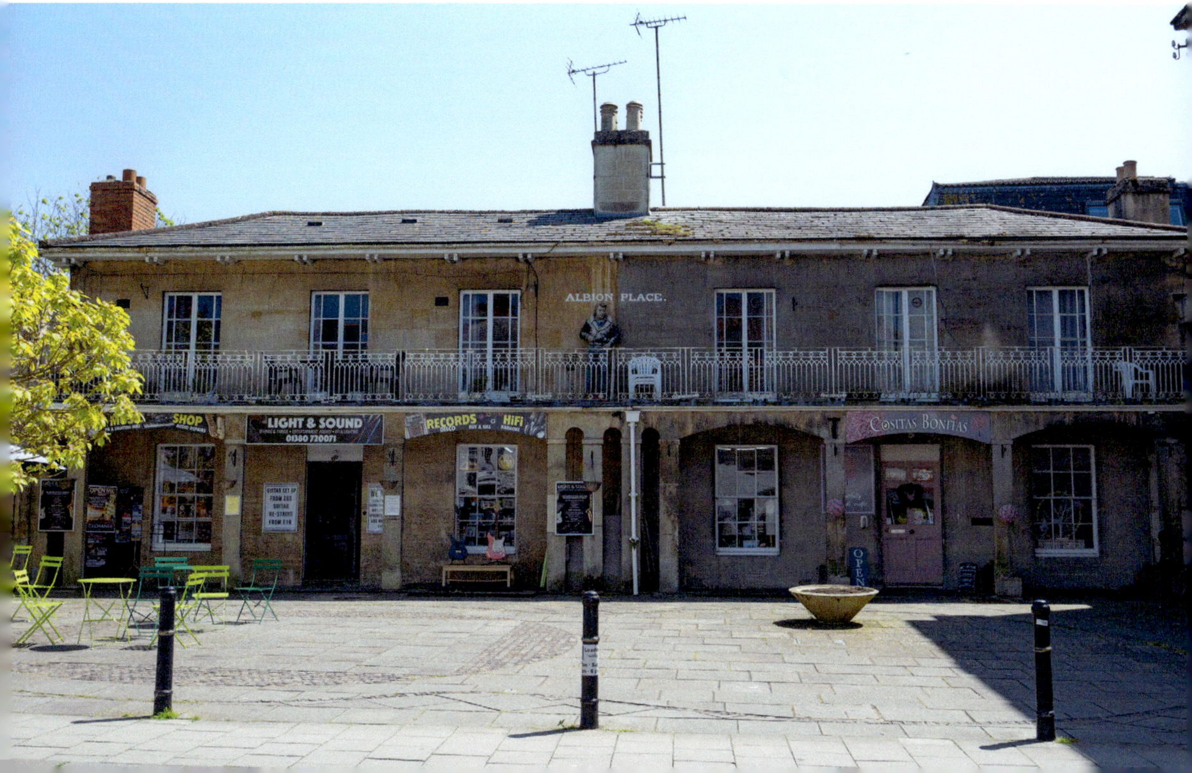

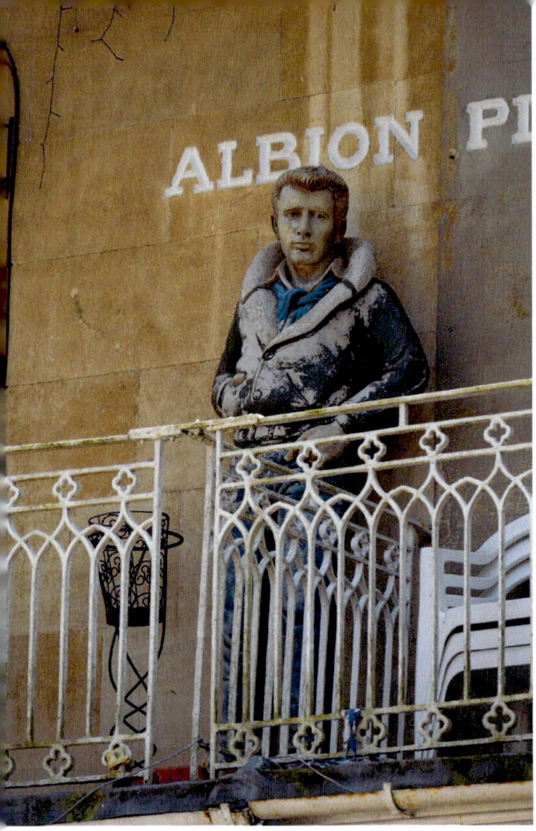

James Dean stares down on Albion Place.

A statue of James Dean was once part of the decor at the Exchange nightclub in the basement of the Corn Exchange, where the owner of Light and Sounds ran the disco. When the nightclub closed its doors, James Dean, along with statues of Elvis and Marilyn Monroe, took up residence on the balcony. Elvis was the first to go – sold to an Elvis impersonator – and the statue of Marilyn Monroe was stolen in 2011, despite weighing some 65 kg. Quite how the thieves managed to make off with the heavy statue has never been established. She was found unexpectedly on Salisbury Plain by a military patrol and delivered back to the store. Unable to reinstall Marilyn in her original location, James Dean now sadly stands alone.

Albion Place was made a listed building in 1954.

Assize Court

The old Devizes Assize Court building stands on Northgate Street, completed in 1835 to a grand Greek Revival design by Thomas Henry Wyatt. The front boasts four remarkable, tall Ionic columns beneath a large portico bearing the coat of arms of the Salisbury family, all finished in traditional warm-coloured Bath stone. At either end of the front of the building stand empty cornices that were intended to house statues that were never installed.

When in use, the judicial processes of the county of Wiltshire were carried out during the spring or summer, depending on the year. At other times the courts were held in Salisbury. By 1899, the County Court for Devizes had also been moved into this purpose-built building which has cells beneath the main courtrooms. Later, a police station was established within the building.

The most famous case heard here was the trial of Rebecca Smith in August 1849. She was found guilty of infanticide and would become the last woman to be executed in the UK. Later, the first meeting of Devizes Council would take place in the Assize Court in January 1889 under John Thynne, 4th Marquess of Bath.

The building became the local Magistrates' Court in 1972, continuing to perform this function until closed by the Lord Chancellor's department during the 1980s. The building then remained empty until 2018 when it was acquired by the newly formed Devizes Assize Court Trust with a view to creating a new home for the Devizes Museum. At the time of writing the building remains magnificent and under restoration. It was awarded a Grade II* listed status in April 1954.

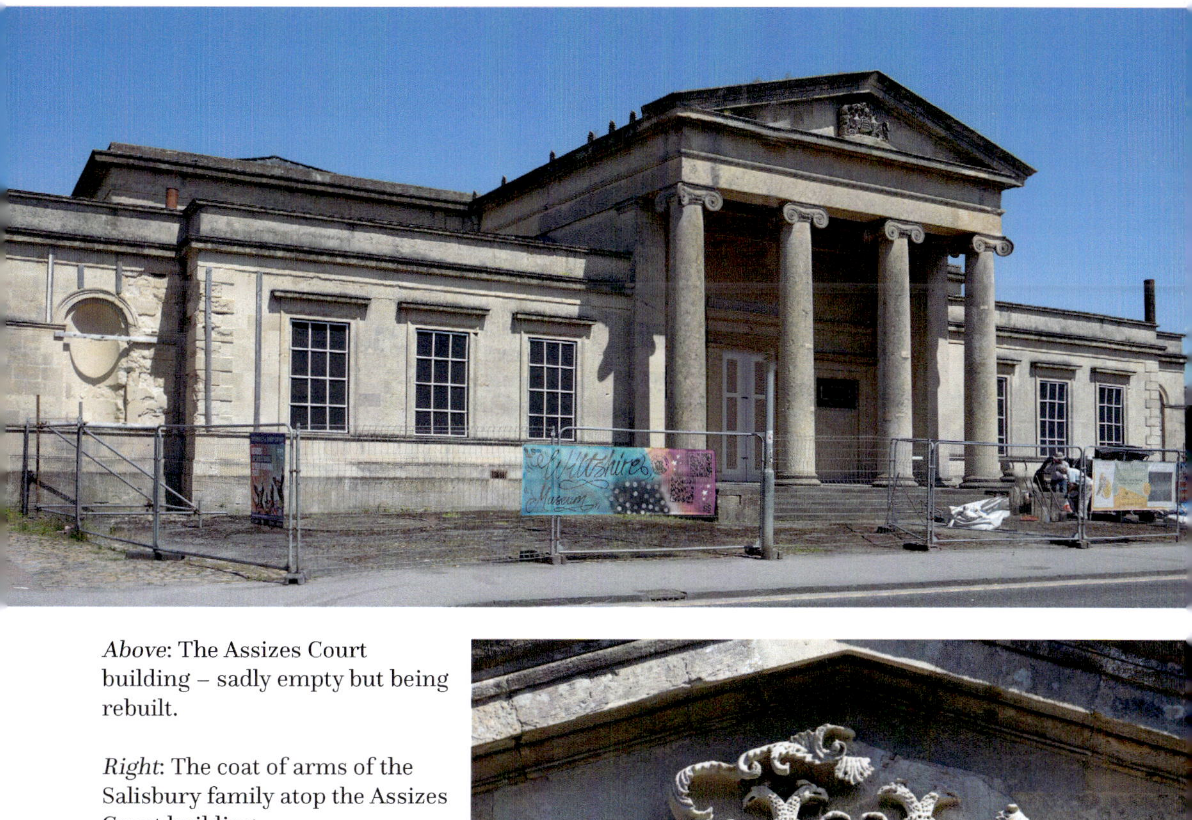

Above: The Assizes Court building – sadly empty but being rebuilt.

Right: The coat of arms of the Salisbury family atop the Assizes Court building.

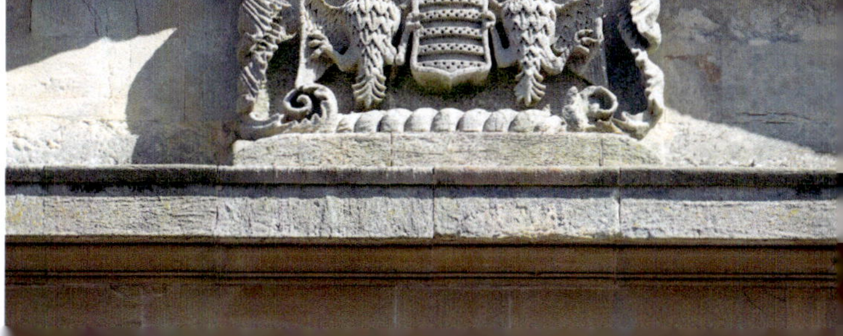

B

Barford House

Barford House, on St John's Street, is just a short walk from both the current Town Hall and the old one. It is a tall, eighteenth-century brick building of striking appearance. English Heritage refer to it as having a 'very fine front'.

Constructed of brick on a stone base, the bricks are arranged in an artistic chequered pattern, with columns of rusticated Bath stone between, running from the top to the bottom of the building. The Bath stone also runs across the top to form a pediment below a final course of red brickwork.

The windows on the ground and first floors have particularly interesting Bath stone frames. They are all topped by a stone pediment and all retain their period sash windows, which is rare to see today.

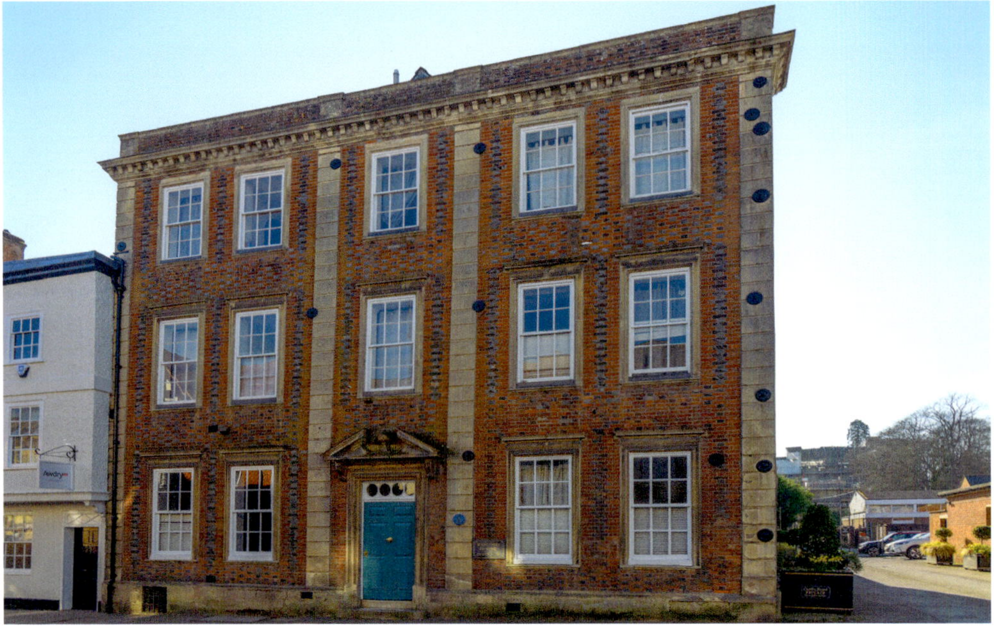

Barford House on St John's Street, a building with a 'very fine frontage'.

The main front door is a fine, tall structure as befitting a building of this style. Above the door are four oval fanlights set into the frame. Surrounding the door is a magnificent (there is no other word for it) stone architrave supporting an unusual triangular pediment above. Where the pediments above a doorway of this period are usually a simple triangle, here it has no upper point – making it technically a broken pediment – but frames a ball within the two ends of the triangle.

The building received listed status in 1970.

Brittox

The Brittox is currently a thriving pedestrianised shopping street, but it was not always thus. In the earliest days of Devizes, when it was still a small settlement around the castle, the Brittox was the only access between the castle and the town – a bridge over the inner town's defensive ditch. The word 'Brittox' itself is believed to be descended from the French word *brattice* meaning a 'wooden stockade', which flanked the roadway. Other sources take the word to mean 'road to the castle', while some believe the name is descended from the French word *bretesque* meaning 'wooden barbican'.

As the years passed and the castle defences became less important, the thoroughfare became a road in its own right, retaining the earlier name.

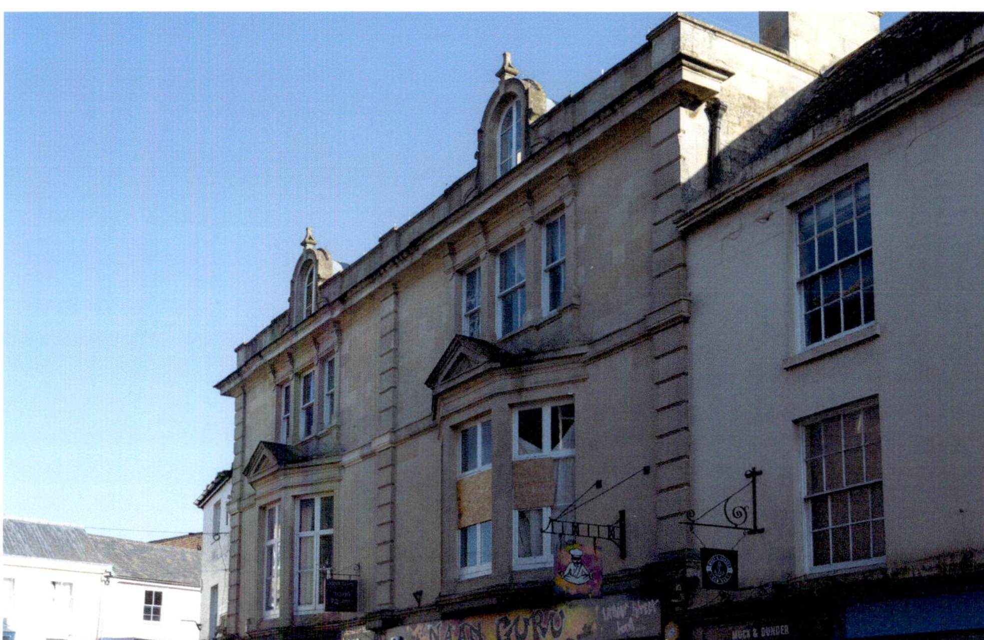

Looking above the modern shopfronts of the Brittox reveals the glories of earlier architecture.

Several of the existing buildings were constructed in the seventeenth and eighteenth centuries and have been listed, though many sadly after they had already been modernised with contemporary shopfronts. Taking a look above the ground level of the shops will reveal a range of interesting details.

Nos 20 and 21 are eighteenth-century buildings, with No. 21 having a nineteenth-century shopfront added. In the early twentieth century, ornate window dividers were installed; taken together, they offer an interesting timeline of retail building development.

Further down at Nos 7, 8 and 9 you will find small eighteenth-century shopfronts that have retained their period three-pane display bay at street level, and a deep cornice still shades the fronts of all three frontages from above. There are four deep sash windows in the main bodies of the whitewashed Bath stone buildings above the shopfronts.

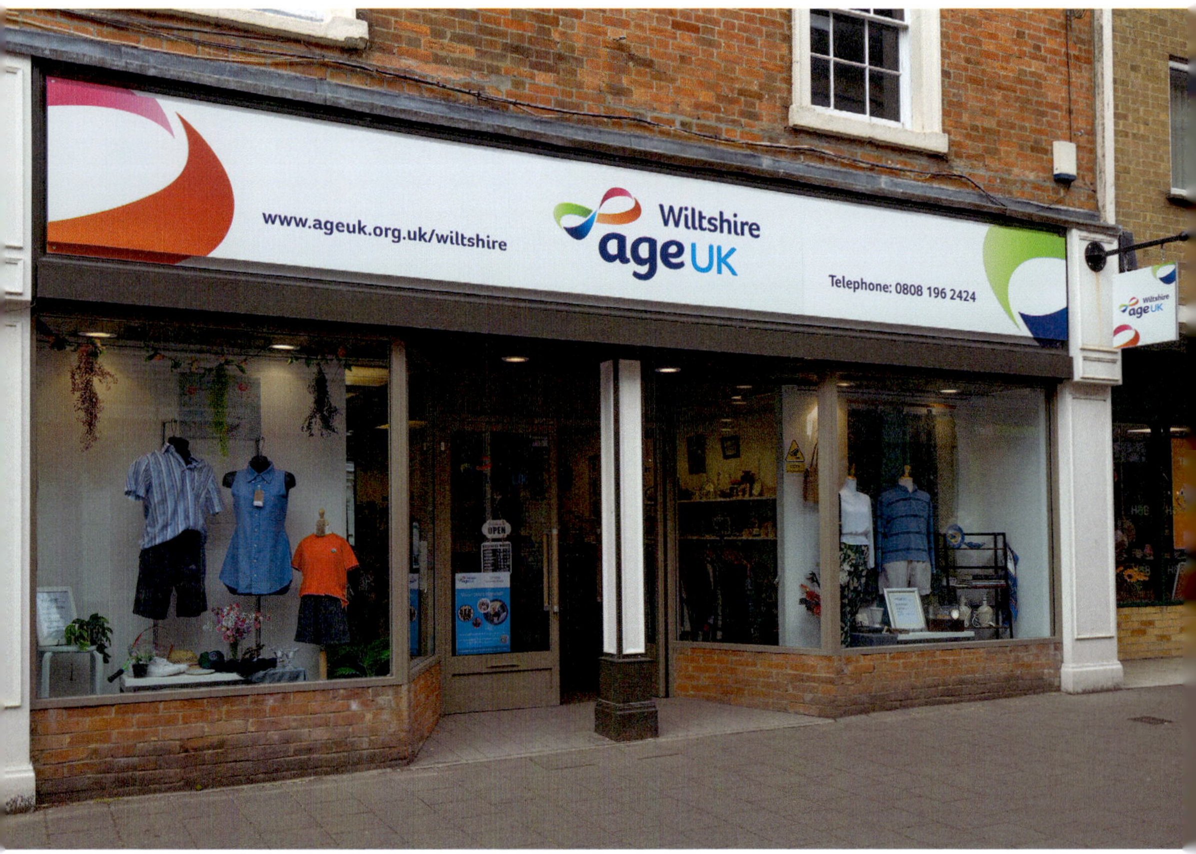

The front pillar and windows of this shop come from a much earlier period.

C

Caen Hill Locks

The Caen Hill Locks (pronounced 'Cane') are a flight of twenty-nine locks (numbered 22–50) on the Kennet and Avon Canal that rise 337 feet over a length of 2 miles. This results in a gradient of 1 in 44 (or 2.2 per cent for those working in metric). On average, it takes between five and six hours to navigate the flight of locks from top to bottom.

The most iconic, and steepest, part of the flight on the approach to Devizes is made up of sixteen locks designed by engineer John Rennie the Elder. These were the last part of the Kennet and Avon Canal to be completed and opened in 1810.

Due to the demands of the building process, a brickyard was created at the bottom of the flight with the sole intention of providing bricks for the construction, though it

The iconic flight of the Caen Locks seen from the lower end.

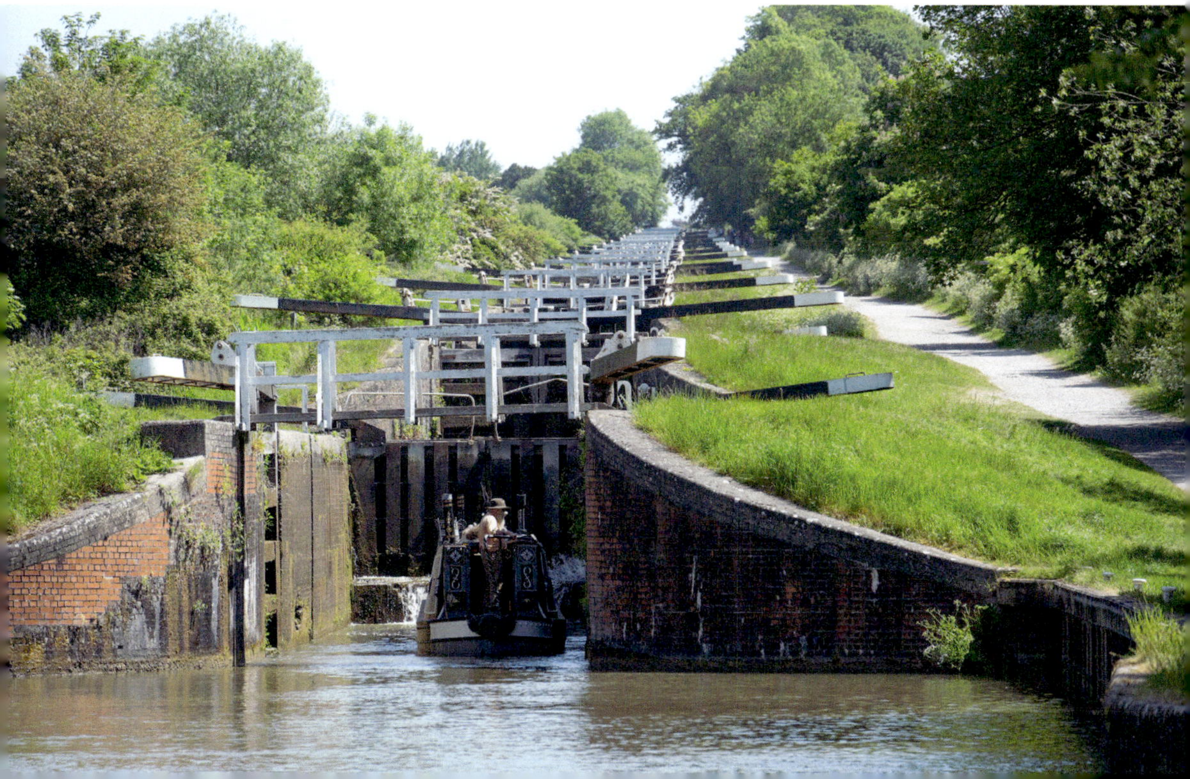

would remain in commercial use well into the 1960s. A small tramway was established to carry bricks and other materials the length of the lock construction site. The tunnels built to accommodate it beneath the bridges over the canal can still be seen today.

Commercial traffic through the locks commenced in 1810 (construction work had begun in 1793) and by 1818 barges of over 76 tons were regularly using the locks to transport coal and stone. On completion, the toll for moving a ton of cargo from London to Bath was £2 9*s* 6*d*, around one-third of what it would have cost to transport the load by road.

Between 1829 and 1849, the locks were lit by gaslight as they were in twenty-four-hour use as a commercial highway. The last commercial cargo passed through the locks in 1948.

The locks fell into disrepair during the 1950s and 1960s. After thirty years' hard work by the Kennet and Avon Canal Trust, Queen Elizabeth II reopened the flight in 1990.

Each lock contains 123,000 litres of water, which is changed every time the lock is filled and emptied (known as a 'lockage'); in a single year around 1,900 lockages take place. Alongside each of the locks is a balancing pond which reduces the amount of water running down the flight of locks during busy periods in the summer. During the average season, no fewer than 2118 Olympic swimming pools' worth of water flows through the locks.

Water is supplied to the locks from several locations. Some comes from the Claverton pumping station between Devizes and Bath, pumping the water no less than 28 km to the locks. Crofton Reservoir (also known as Wilton Water) produces

Every canal lock has a unique number; Caen Locks cover the numbers 22 to 50.

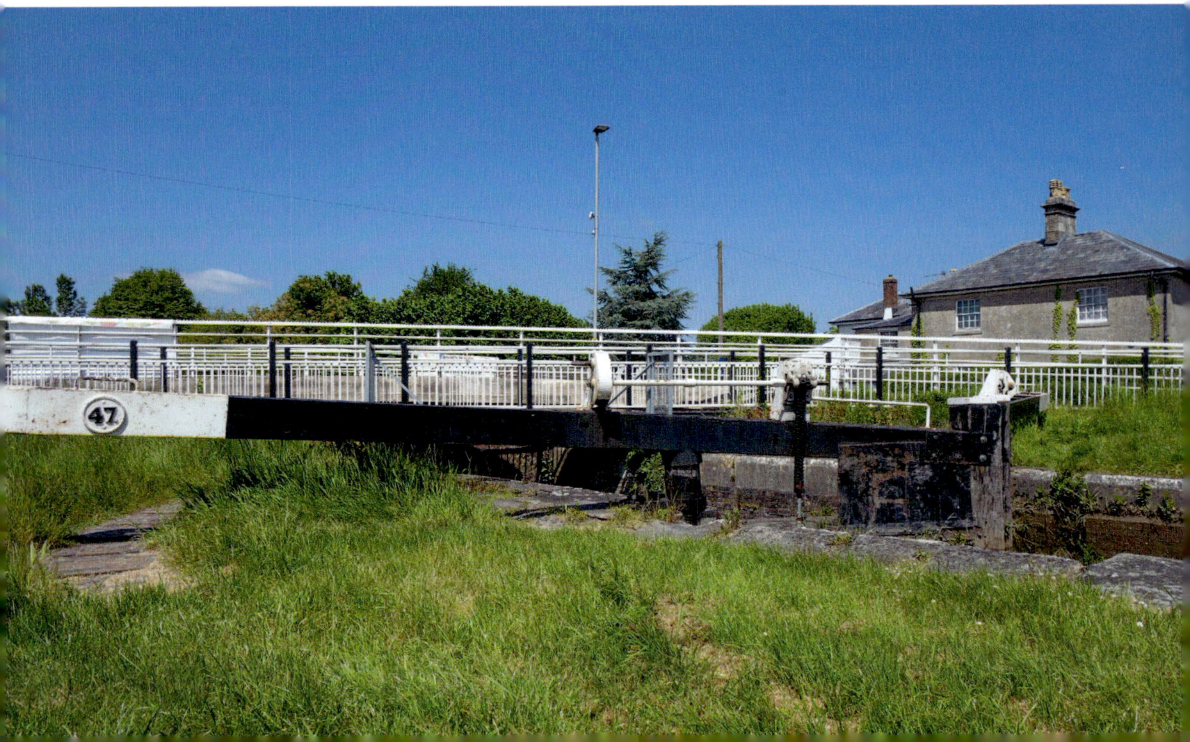

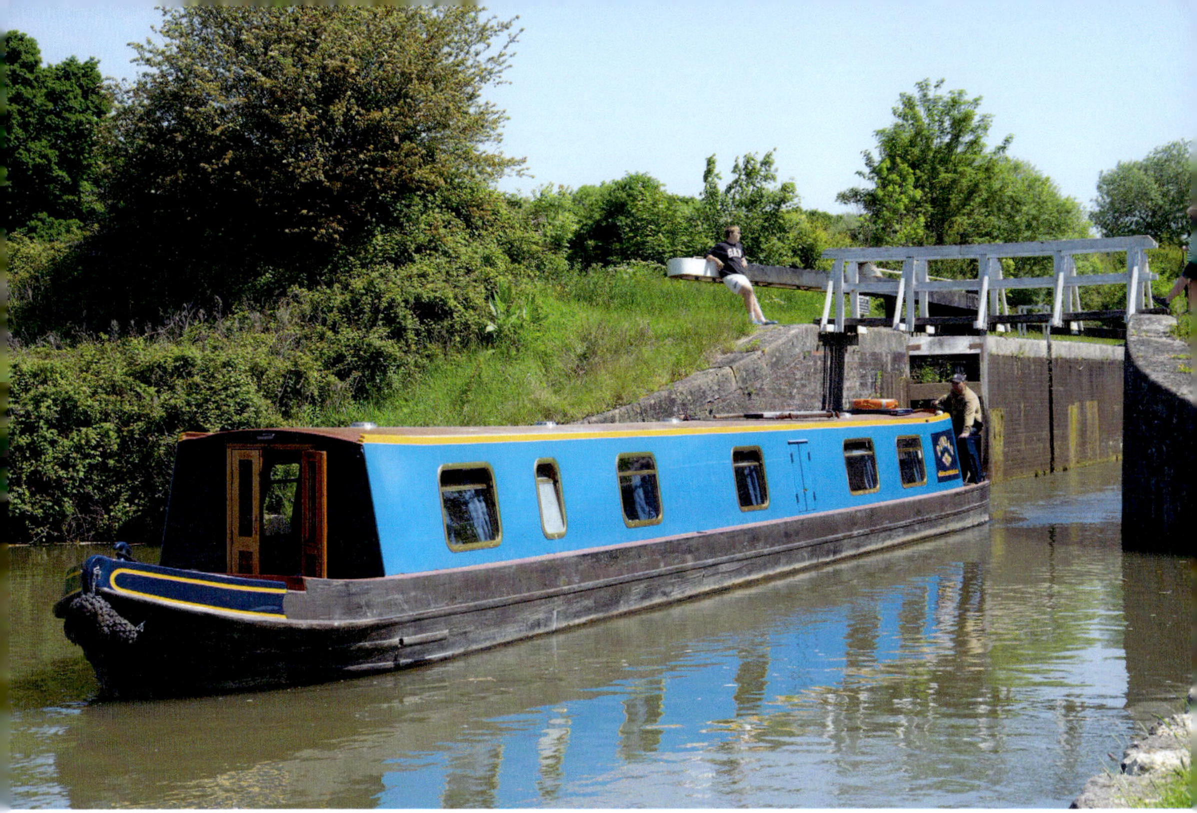

Above: The locks are wide enough for two traditional narrowboats to enter.

Below: Towpath tunnels for the movement of bricks still exist.

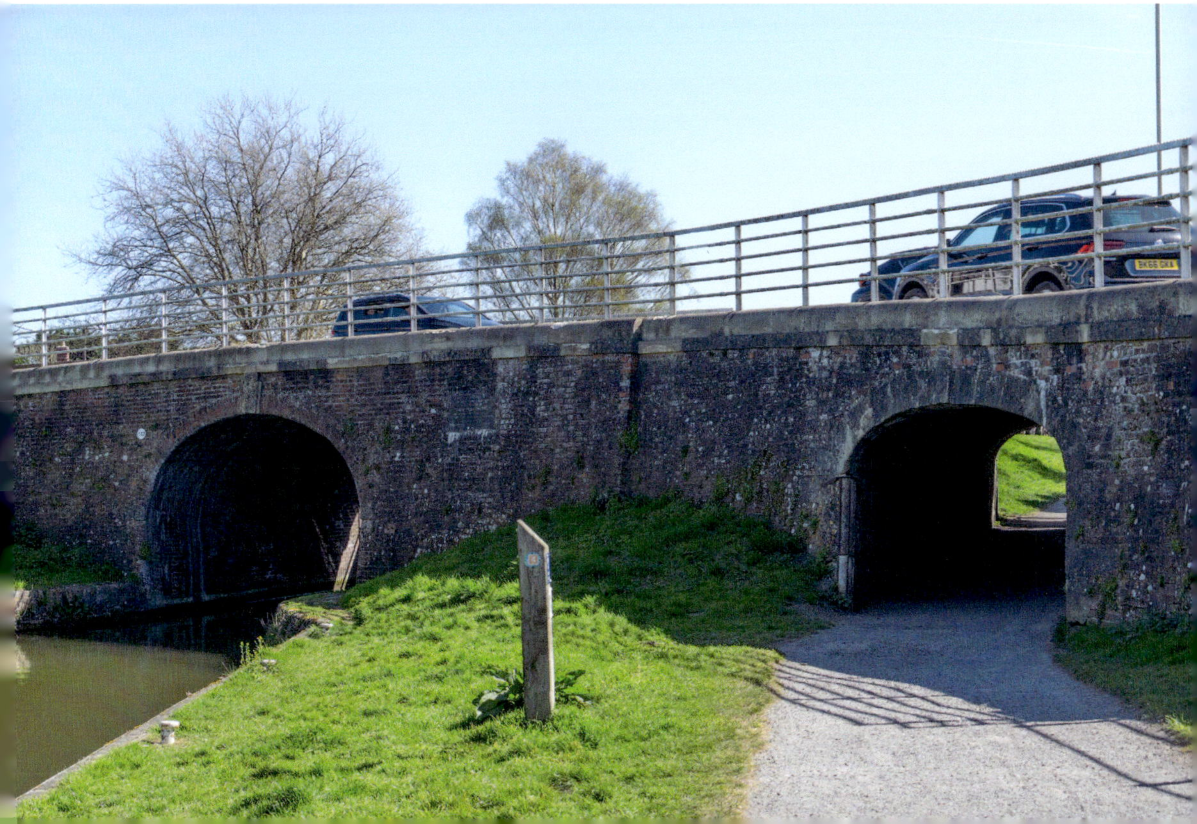

a natural supply to what is known as the Summit Pond, which is otherwise filled by pumped water. A Boulton and Watt pumping engine was installed for this purpose in 1812, and a Harvey's engine was installed alongside it in 1815. Both were rebuilt in 1987 and the Boulton and Watt engine supplies water to this day.

A new, modern pump was installed at Foxhangers in 1996 which is capable of pumping 7 million imperial gallons up the entire flight of locks every day to keep them running smoothly at peak times. At the very top of the flight stands the Caen Hill Café, where many a wandering tourist and boat crewman has stopped to refill their personal physical reserves.

Informally known as one of the 'seven wonders of the waterways', Caen Hill Locks are a Scheduled Ancient Monument under the Ancient Monuments and Archaeological Areas Act 1979.

Castle Hotel

The Castle Hotel is an eighteenth-century brick-built coaching inn that stands on the corner of New Park Street and Castle Road in the centre of town. Spread over three floors, it is famed for the roaring fire in the depths of winter and its splendid restaurant.

It was built to service the needs of travellers on the new southern turnpike road that joined Bath and London. It is believed to have been constructed after the White Bear Hotel, located opposite, with the aim of being more attractive to wealthier travellers who wanted more modern facilities.

The building is an unusual 'L' shape and backs onto the entrance to the churchyard of St Mary's Church. Two original stable blocks stand to the north of the main building from the days when travellers arrived on horseback or in their own carriages. One displays a magnificent fan window facing the main road and both have retained the large archways required to allow access to the stable yard for horse-drawn vehicles. Thankfully, they remain open and have not been bricked over by later developments.

The main entrance to the Castle Hotel has a magnificent period architrave cover supported by a pair of stone Doric columns and often sports a covering of seasonal flowers above. On the corner of the building a traditional inn sign hangs from an ornate period metal frame rather than the more typical pole. The sign harks back to the early days of the town and shows a romanticised image of the original Devizes Castle.

Mounted high on the wall of the Castle Hotel is a curious logo depicting a wheel with three wings intertwined in the spokes. This is the symbol of the Cyclists Touring Club and was often prominently displayed on the side of pubs and hotels where their custom was welcome. Though no longer a common sight, it still appears on several public houses across the Cotswolds.

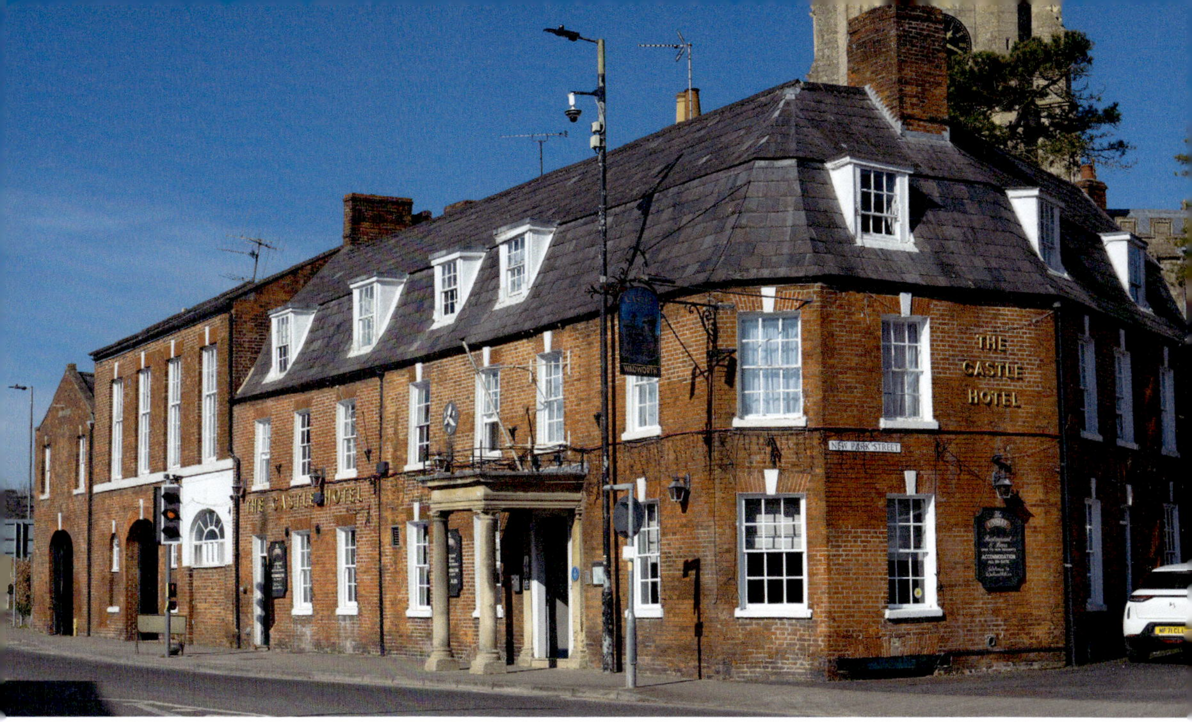

Above: The Castle Hotel stands on Castle Road and New Park Street.

Below left: The romanticised Castle Hotel sign hangs on an ornate iron frame.

Below right: The sign of the Cyclist Touring Club, indicting cyclists were welcome from 1883.

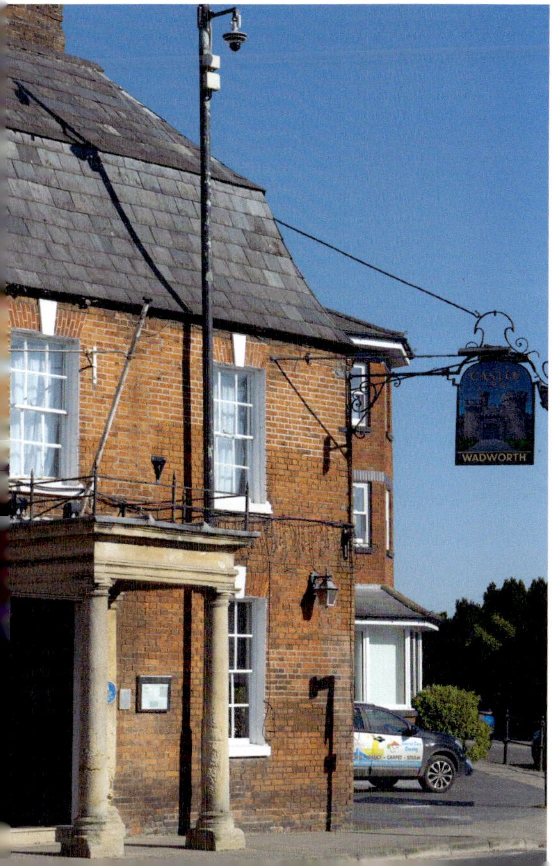

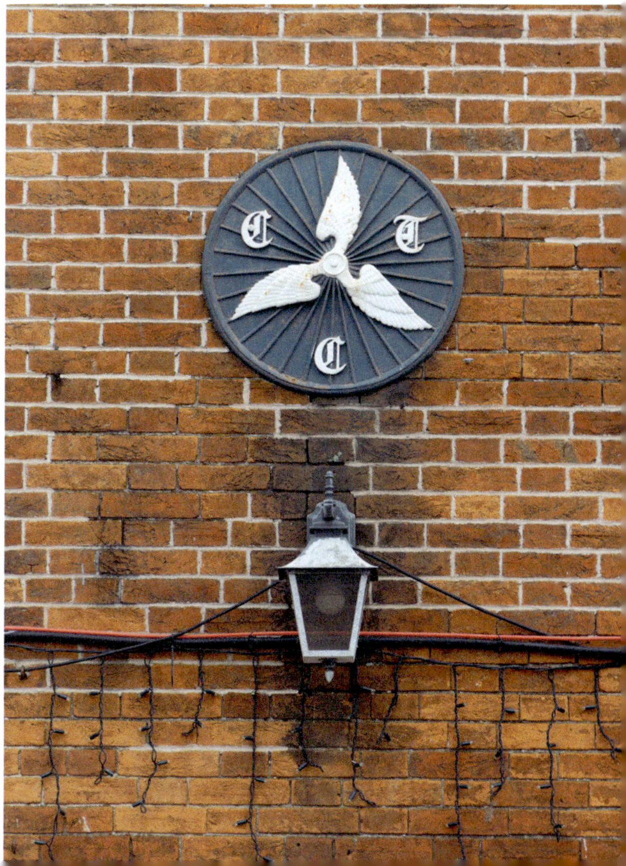

Formed in 1878 as the Bicycle Touring Club, they became the Cyclists Touring Club in 1883, when the logo seen here was introduced. The organisation lasted until 2016, when it became known as Cycling UK.

The Castle serves the locally brewed Wadworth beer and, as it stands close to the brewery, if you are lucky, you might spot their beer being delivered by the brewery's own Shire horse-drawn dray.

As with many of the more famous buildings in Devizes, it was awarded listed status in 1954.

Corn Exchange

Designed by W. Hill of Leeds in a neoclassical style and built by John Rendall of Devizes, the Corn Exchange opened for business in 1897. It stands on Market Place facing the Shambles Market and the magnificent Market Cross.

Constructed of local Bath stone, the front-facing Market Place is resplendent with four Corinthian columns and three arched doorways with flanking arched windows. Above the central of the three doors is a rendition of the Norman Devizes Castle, which led to the foundation of the town. Above that are three carved bosses featuring the goods that would once have been traded there; the central one, featuring ears of corn, is the most prominent.

The Corn Exchange on the Market Place.

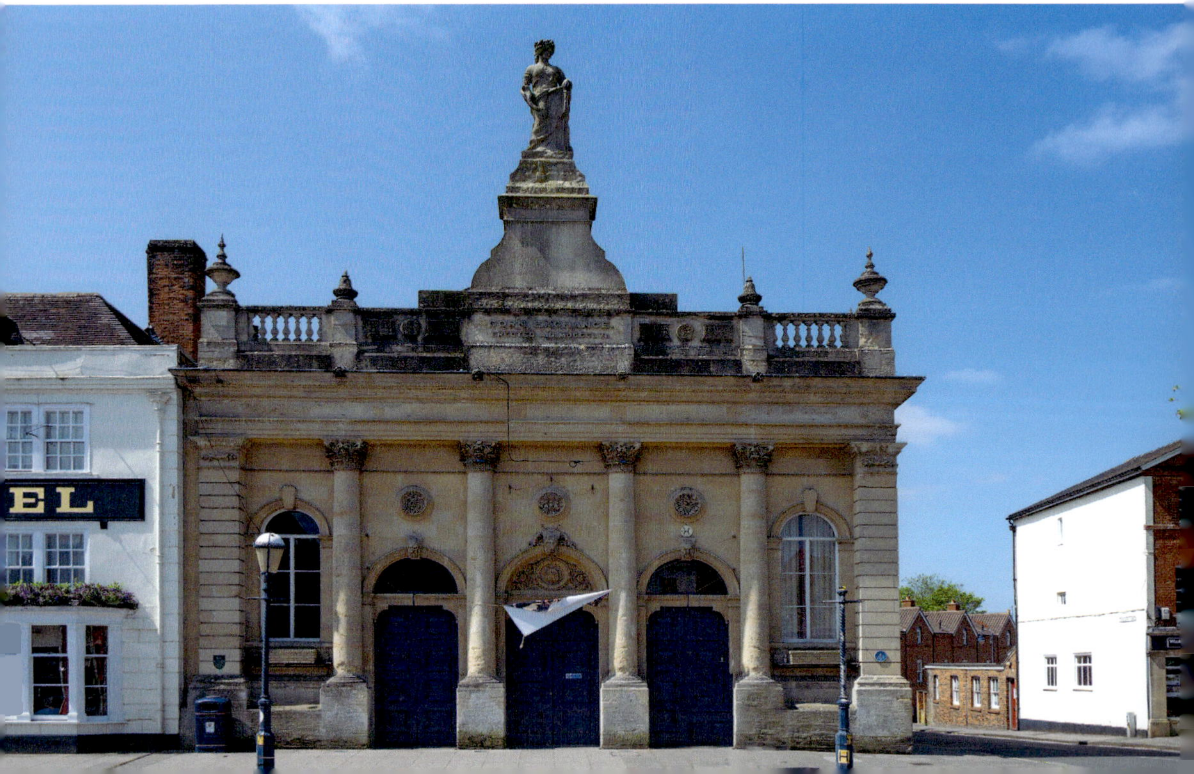

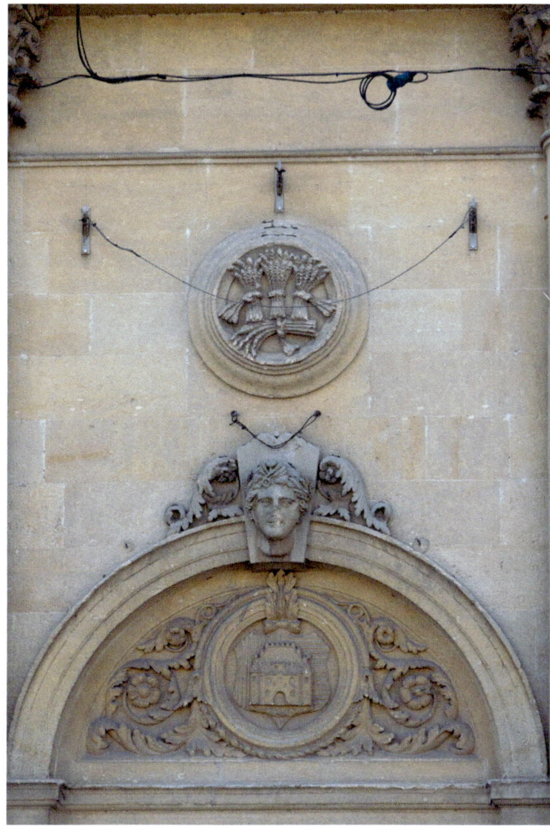

This carved stone boss on the Corn Exchange depicts the ears of corn once traded there.

Atop the building is a tall statue of the Roman goddess Ceres, goddess of agriculture, grains and harvest, fertility and motherhood. She is depicted clutching her traditional horn of plenty and looks down to keep a vigil over Market Place.

Prior to the building of the Corn Exchange, Devizes was the home of the largest grain market in the area, and farmers traded in the open. Sacks were loaded around the Market Cross and trading took place in the fresh air.

In the early nineteenth century, local counsellors decided to create a more formal indoor space for trading to take place. The site of the old Bear Assembly Rooms was selected as the ideal location. The Assembly Rooms were demolished and rebuilt at the rear of the Bear Hotel, which now stands alongside the Corn Exchange. The new building cost £3,456 to build and was opened by Mayor Henry Butcher on 3 December 1857.

Following the Great Depression in British agriculture of the late nineteenth century, the Corn Exchange became known as a performance venue. Many well-known pop groups performed there much later during the 1970s and 1980s, including the Who, Thin Lizzy and Dr Feelgood.

There is a small plaque by the main doors of the building showing thanks from local farms to the Women's Land Army, who worked the farms in the area during the Second World War while the men were away fighting.

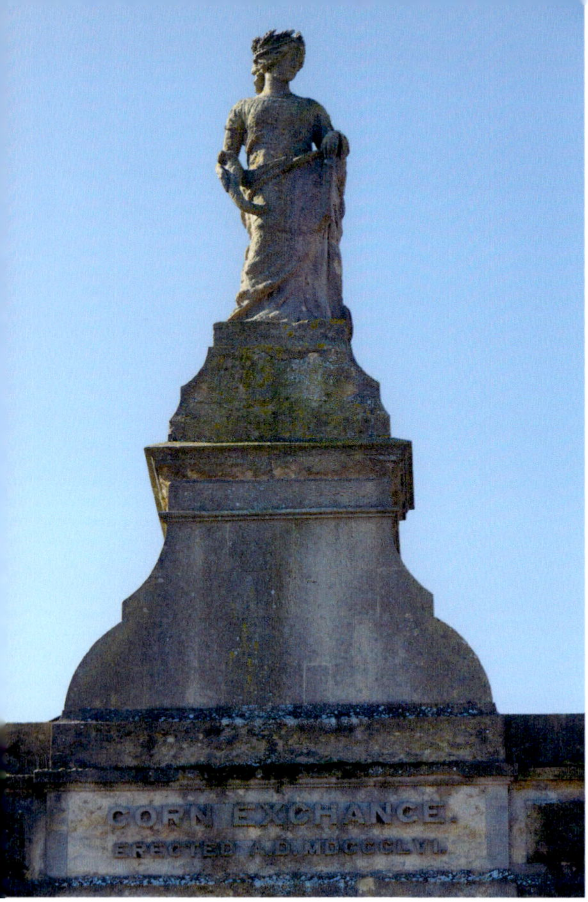

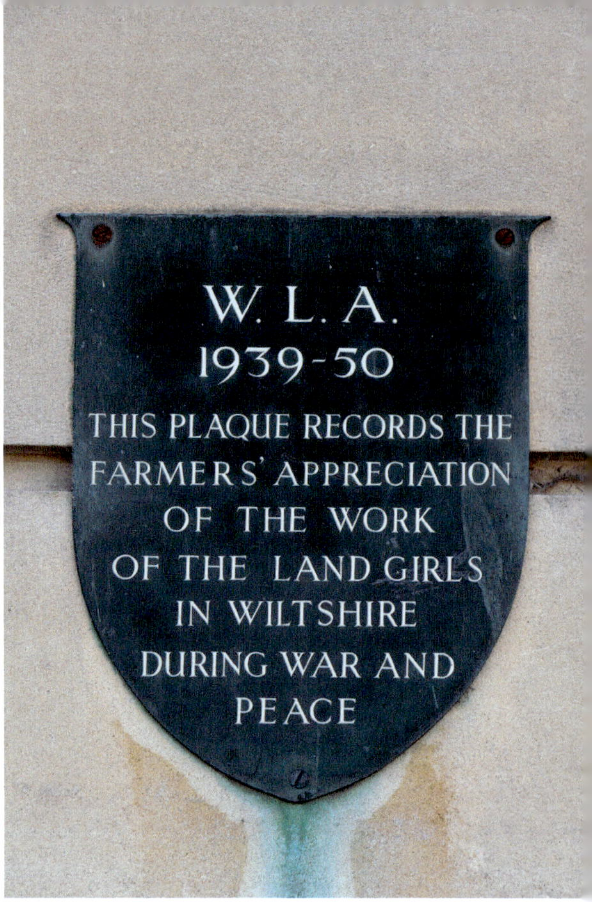

Above left: The figure of the goddess Ceres standing atop the Corn Exchange.

Above right: Plaque commemorating the work of the Women's Land Army in Wiltshire.

The condition of the building declined during the 1980s and large-scale restoration took place during the 1990s. It was formally reopened by local MP Sir Charles Morrison on 3 May 1995 as a performance venue and social space for Devizes.

Now operated by the council, the once vast trading rooms have become function suites and rooms for hire. The rooms are named after earlier uses of the building and include Ceres Hall and the Wessex and Yeoman room, named after the local regiment. Beneath the main building lurks the Exchange nightclub and their private venue, the Merchants Room.

The Corn Exchange was awarded listed status in April 1954.

Crammer

Adjoining the popular open space of Devizes green is a large pond called the Crammer. The first reference to it with this name is on Dore's map of Devizes dated 1759. There is some discussion as to where the name originates. Some believe it comes from travelling German merchants – *kramer* – who would set up their stalls around the pond to sell their wares, while others believe it derives from the word *cranmere* meaning 'crane pond'.

A later 1840 map shows it as being slightly smaller since some of it was filled in when the churchyard of St James' Church was expanded.

Local legend has it that the Crammer is the source of the 'Moonraker' legend. According to the legend, a group of men from the nearby village of Bishops Cannings were being pursued by local government excise officers whilst in possession of contraband brandy, which they hid by dropping it into the water. When they returned later to retrieve their goods they were approached by the officials, who had spotted them trawling the water with large agricultural rakes. On being challenged, they are said to have replied that they were 'trying to get that girt big cheese out of the water' while pointing at the reflection of the moon on the pond. The excise officers are said to have ridden off chuckling at the foolishness and stupidity of the locals. Now alone, the men were able to retrieve their contraband and make off with it undisturbed.

Over the years, there have been several prospective development projects that have threatened the site of the Crammer, such as the construction of a wall for health and safety reasons. Devizes Trades Council even wished to drain it in 1953 and turn the space into a car park and bus terminus. This led to the formation of the Trust for Devizes, a body that has campaigned for the preservation of the historic local area ever since.

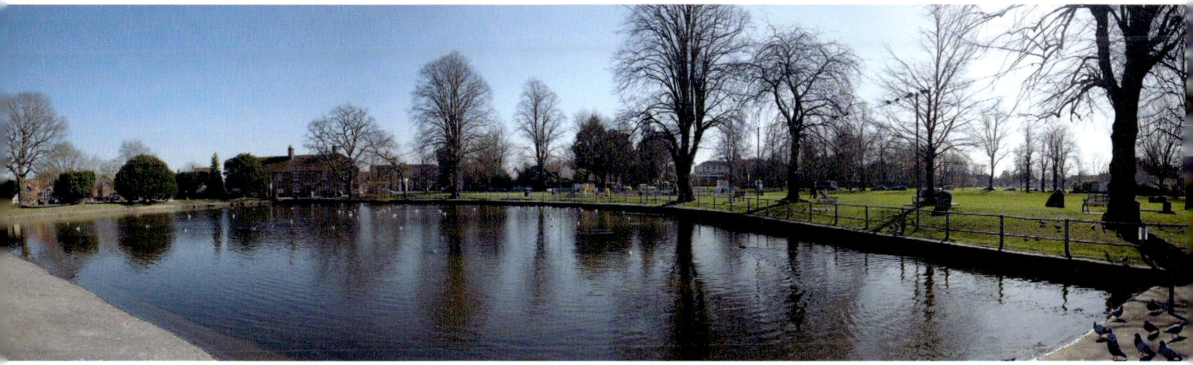

The Crammer by the green.

D

Diamond Jubilee Wood

The Caen Hill Diamond Jubilee Wood is one of sixty planted around the UK in 2012 in commemoration of the diamond jubilee of Queen Elizabeth II.

Accessed from the tow footpath that runs alongside the Caen Hill Locks, the woods stand on the site of a long-disused pig farm and were created through the planting of trees supplied by the forestry commission.

Four disused and derelict ponds were located and rather than spend huge amounts of funds restoring them, a fresh pond was created to add to the desired wildlife diversity the wood would create.

Diamond Jubilee Wood.

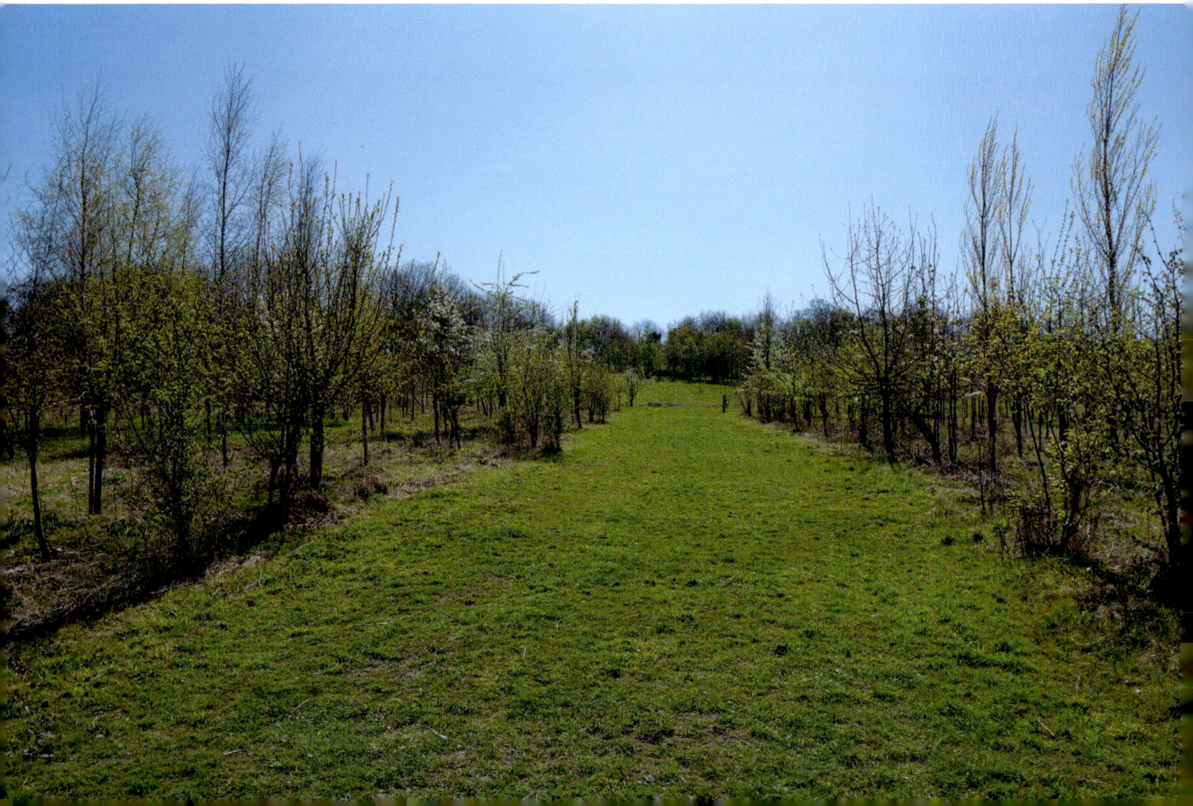

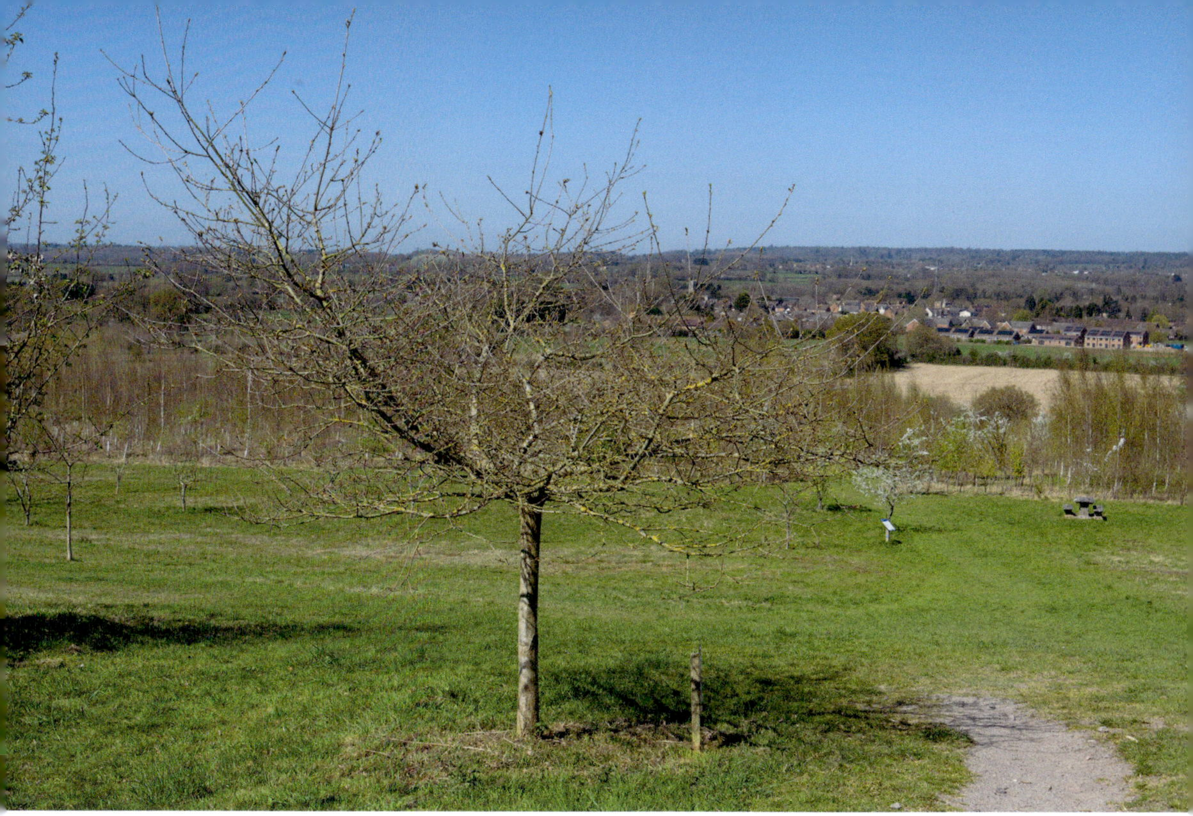

The Royal Oak at the entrance to the Diamond Jubilee Wood.

The oak parkland was created by planting a mixture of mature oaks and saplings, with the hope that in time a diverse oak woodland will grow. As oak trees have a predicted lifespan of over 100 years, future generations will be able to enjoy the results of this planting. They can also enjoy the wildlife diversity they attract; a single mature oak tree can support 2,000 species of wildlife.

At the entrance to the oak parkland stands the Royal Oak. Grown from an acorn gathered from a very old oak tree that stands in Windsor Great Park, it was the final tree planted in the woodland, and was planted by local MP Claire Perry.

E

Estcourt Street

Running up one side of the green and alongside the watery delights of the Crammer is Estcourt Street. Once called Bedbury Street, it is now home to a number of listed buildings, the architectural style of which vary remarkably as you walk along it. At one end stands the delightful St James' Church and both ends of Estcourt Crescent open on to it.

Estcourt Crescent itself is made up of three ornate, separate red-brick terraces of differing styles built for the workers of Devizes. One terrace has each doorway and window topped by a stone lintel, while the two later terraces have courses of dark-coloured bricks running horizontally through the brickwork and raising over both doors and windows in emulation of the older terrace.

The differing terraces of Estcourt Terrace.

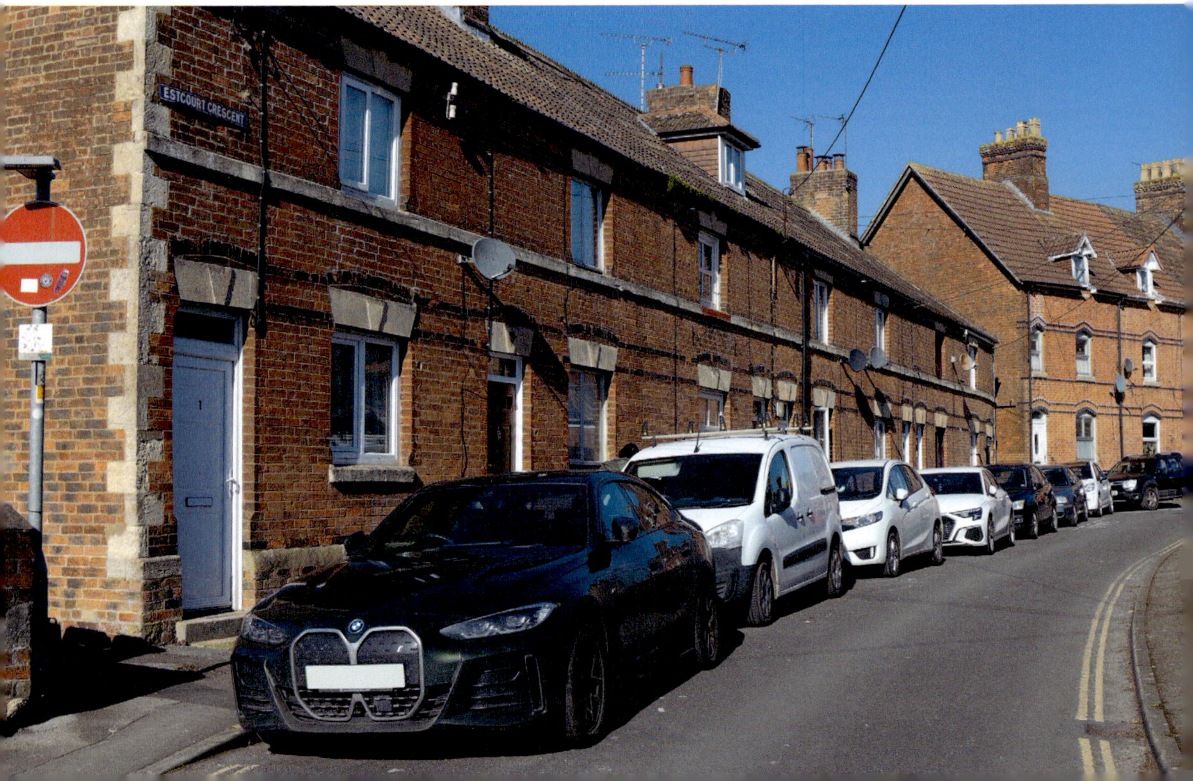

Estcourt Street is now part of the main A361 trunk road through Devizes and is far busier than it once was, but a walk allows you to take in the various architectural styles at leisure.

Next door to the hustle and bustle of Kwik-Fit (on the site of the older Blue Star garage) stands the ornate brickwork of Victoria Cottage. A fine stone statue of Queen Victoria once stood here before being moved outside Kwik-Fit. After its third episode of vandalism and decapitation in thirteen years it was removed to the grounds of St Mary's almshouses on the nearby, and aptly named, Victoria Road. The last missing head of the statue was later recovered and showed sign of having been used as a football. The incidents of broken toes or mighty boots that must have resulted from this game of football makes the mind boggle.

A fresh head, financed by Kwik-Fit, was sculpted by local stonemason Geoffrey Stephenson, which was arguably more accurate and certainly more greatly resembled the classic stamp and coin image of Queen Victoria.

Just down the road stands the Bell Inn, which used to stand next door to the brewhouse of the Estcourt brewery. Run by the Wild family, it supplied beer directly to the Bell, among others, and would eventually be bought out by Wadworth just down the road. While the brewery building was demolished during the 1980s, the landlord of the Bell Inn has been heard to say that the cellars of the old brewery still exist under the new Morrisons car park.

The Bell Inn is a fascinating-looking late eighteenth-century building, having two pronounced, rounded bays on the front of the building faced with Bath stone. There

The Bell Inn.

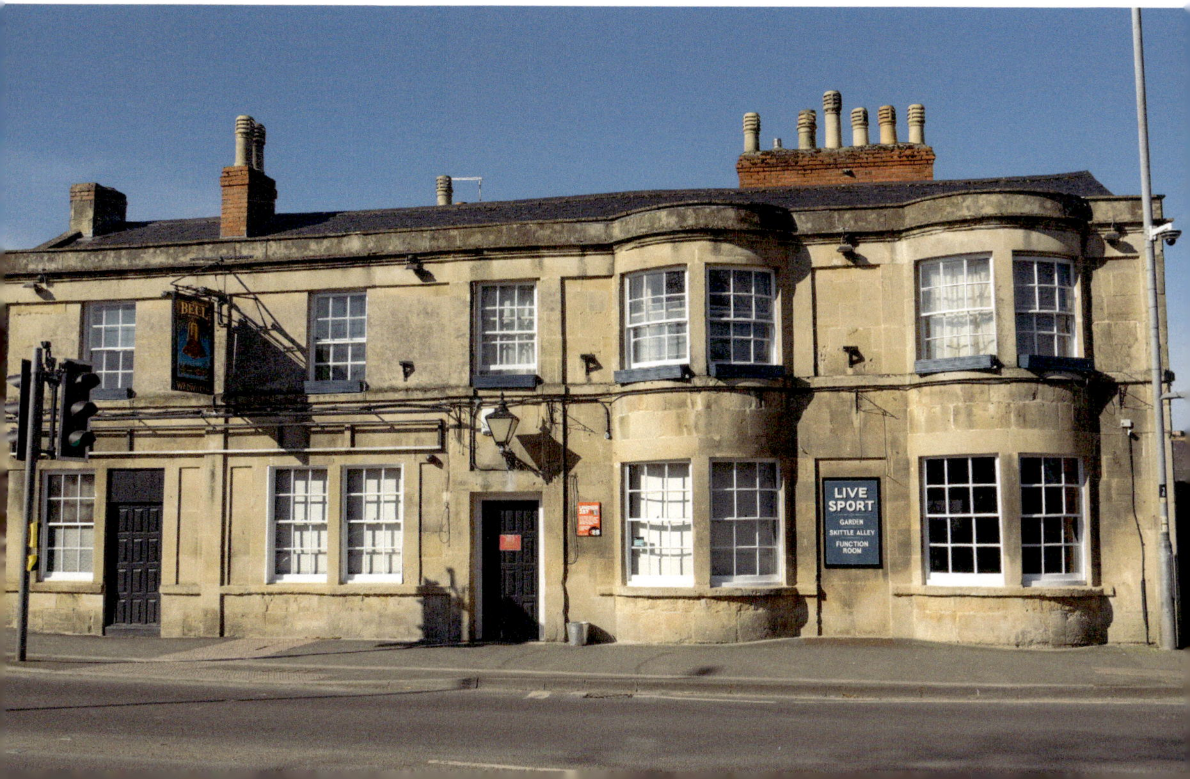

are two inscriptions carved on the building. One reads, 'Wines, sprits and ales'; the other, 'Fear God and honour the Queen'. As with much of Devizes, the Bell is a listed building, being made so in 1972.

Just across the roundabout from the pub stands the B&M brick terrace dated 1874. Both labels were inscribed on diamond-shaped blocks of Bath stone above unusual semicircular doorways and ornamented with two contrasting colours of brickwork. Just along the road are two more pleasing brick-built terraces, one clearly younger than the other. The first you reach is a more modern affair, while the next is the far grander Estcourt Terrace, built in 1874. It stands three storeys high with lead-roofed bay windows and fine triangular features in the roof space.

At the end of the road is the Southbroom schoolhouse, another grand Bath-stone-faced building with a long-decayed and weathered motto above the former front entrance. It remains in use as a school to this day, though pupils now enter from the rear. Opposite is the grandeur of St James' Church, of which more later.

The street itself is named after Devizes MP Thomas Henry Sutton Estcourt, whose memorial fountain stands in the Market Place outside the Shambles Market.

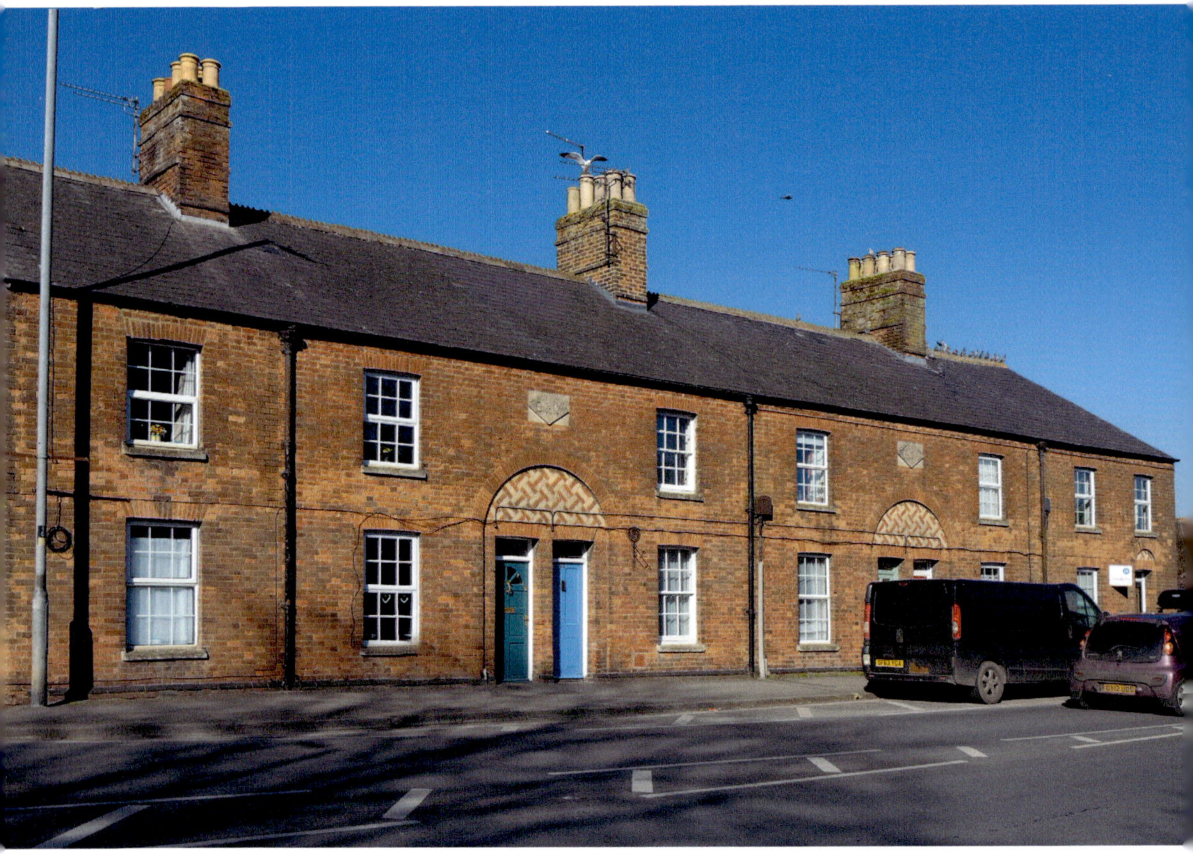

An ornate terrace on Estcourt Street.

F

Fanny Duberly

Fanny Duberly was born in Brownston House on New Park Street in Devizes in 1829. She was the daughter of the politician Wadham Locke and in 1845 she married Captain Henry Duberly, paymaster of the 8th Royal Irish Hussars, part of the British light cavalry establishment. Remarkably for the time, rather than staying at home in England she accompanied her husband on his postings with the army and wrote journals about her travels and experiences.

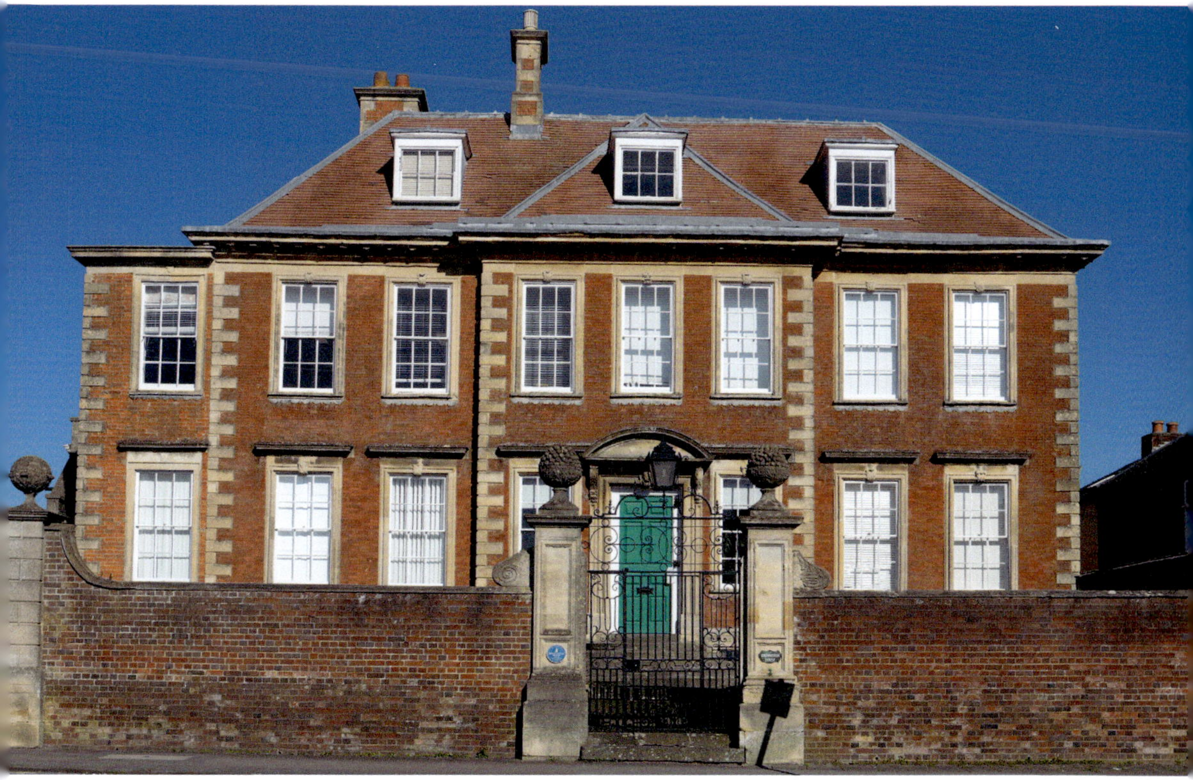

Brownston House, once home of Fanny Duberly.

She joined him to the Crimean War where, despite objections by the British commanding officer Lord Lucan, she was the only officer's wife to travel to the front and witness first-hand the realities of battle. Reportedly well liked by the officers and displaying a degree of toughness and an aptitude for the rough soldiering life, she was often permitted to watch battles from locations close to the action. She witnessed the Battle of Balaclava first-hand, including the actions of her husband's regiment at the infamous Charge of the Light Brigade. She lost many friends at Balaclava and declined to view the aftermath of the Battle of Inkerman, fearing it would make her sick.

She published her experiences upon her return under the title *Journal Kept During the Russian War* in 1855, which also famously included rumours and gossip she had heard while on campaign. She was photographed on horseback in 1855 by famous Crimean War photographer Roger Fenton. Upon the publication of her journal he found himself with a steady demand for prints of this image, a testament to her popularity in England.

In 1865, Fanny accompanied her husband on campaign again, this time to India during the First War of Indian Independence, sailing from Cork on the SS *Great Britain*, famously designed by Isambard Kingdom Brunel. Her husband's regiment saw action in the latter parts of the war and Fanny inadvertently took part in a cavalry charge at Gwalior in June 1858 when her horse bolted after the charging cavalry.

The Duberlys returned to England in 1864 and Fanny's husband eventually rose to the rank of Lieutenant Colonel of the army's pay department, passing away in 1890. Fanny died in 1902 and was buried alongside her husband in the churchyard of St Peter's in Leckhampton, Cheltenham.

G

Gazette and Herald

Established in 1816 as the *Devizes and Wiltshire Gazette*, their original Market Place offices still proudly display the original hand-painted sign on the front of the building, despite the paper now being based in Swindon. Below the upper residential floors is Mikey's Barber Shop, winner of the 'Most Outstanding Effort of a Small Business Premises' award in 2015.

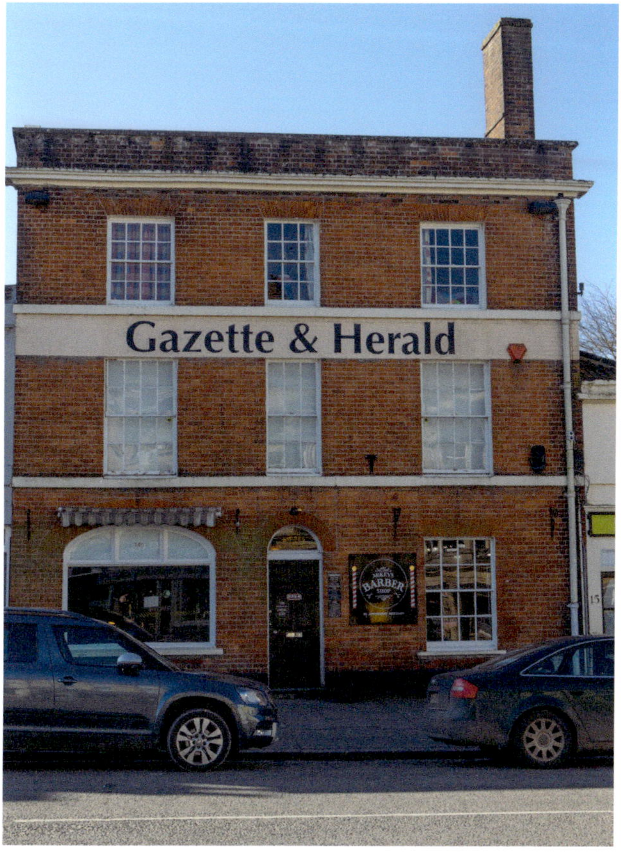

The Gazette and Herald building still wears its logo with pride.

The paper's main offices were moved to Swindon in 1920 when it was purchased by the Swindon press group. The *Gazette* was then merged with other papers owned by them, most notably the *North Wiltshire Herald*.

In 1956, the *Devizes and Wiltshire Gazette* was officially renamed the *Gazette and Herald* and began to be published in six distinct editions every Thursday to cover different areas (Malmesbuy, Chippenham, Calne, Devizes, Marlborough and Swindon) but retaining a single title, a system that exists to this day. Audited figures currently claim a readership of over 70,000 per copy. *The Wiltshire Times*, its sister paper under the same ownership, covers those parts of Wiltshire not reached by the *Gazette and Herald*.

Unusually for a local paper, a large selection of early issues have survived and are available for viewing in digital form at the National Newspaper Archive, the earliest being the edition for 2 May 1822.

Readers travelling into the northern reaches of Yorkshire may be surprised to see their local paper on sale in Ryedale, near Scarborough. Closer examination will reveal that, in one of those coincidences of life, this is another local paper of exactly the same title.

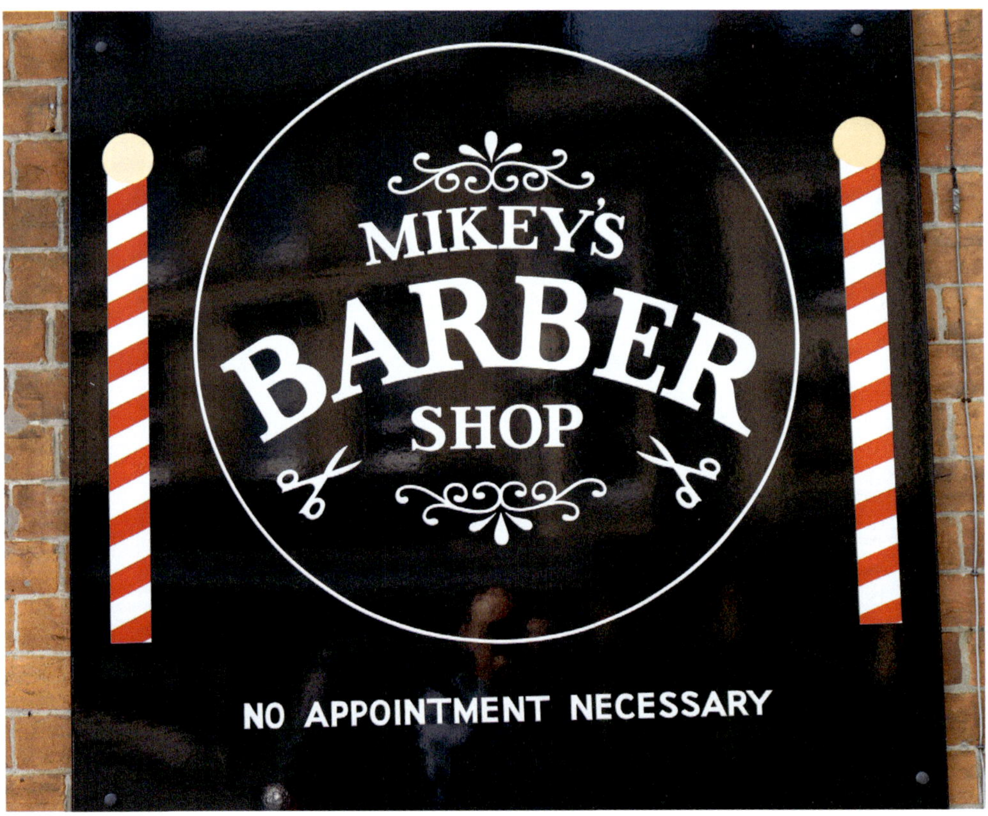

Mikey's award-winning barber shop stands below the Gazette and Herald sign.

George Eliot

Famous British author George Eliot (a woman by the name of Mary Ann Evans), author of such books as *Silas Marner* and *The Mill on the Floss*, briefly stayed in Devizes in 1843 at a house called Sandcliff on Northgate Street.

Still a young person of twenty-four, she had accepted the invitation to stay with the family of a friend, Rufa Brabant. Her friend's father, Dr Robert Brabant, was a leading citizen of Devizes and practising doctor. He had invited the author to stay after meeting her at his daughter's wedding and found they had a common interest in German theology. For reasons that have never been fully explained, the visit was cut short. Robert Brabant is rumoured to have formed the basis for the character of Revd Edward Casubond in her novel *Middlemarch*.

George Eliot returned to Devizes in 1874 when she was searching for material and locations for what would be her final, and arguably less well-known, novel, *Daniel Deronda*, published in 1876. This time she stayed at the Bear Hotel and came away with a wealth of material, such as Lacock Abby that was the pattern for Topping Abby, Bowood would become Diplow and Corsham Court would become Brackewnshaw.

Sandcliff House, the location of her first visit, would continue to be the home of a doctor until 1988 when local physician Dr John Siggers passed away. Fascinated by the earlier visit of George Eliot to his home, he made a hobby of studying her and her work and accumulated a large amount of material on the subject. On his passing,

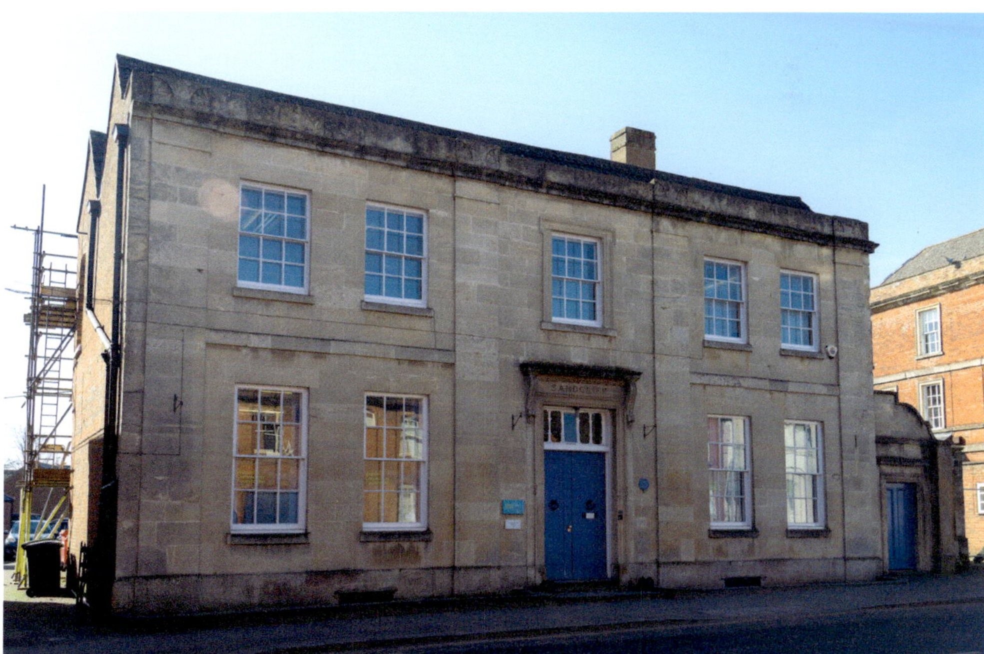

Sandcliff House, where George Eliot stayed during her first visit to Devizes.

it was donated to the local Wiltshire museum. He was also famous for his detailed study of Wiltshire postmarks, the collection of which also now resides in the nearby museum. Today a blue plaque is placed on the house in memory of Eliot's visit.

Great Porch House

Standing on the northern corner of Monday Market Street is the striking black-timbered frame of Great Porch House, which can lay claim to being one of the oldest buildings in Devizes. The original structure was built in the fifteenth century – the board on the front of the building lists a date of 1450. The much later nineteenth-century building of white brickwork with cosmetic white timbers is now joined to it and is part of the same building. It is one of only two surviving medieval buildings in Devizes, narrowly escaping demolition in 1954 when a relief road was proposed for Monday Market Street. It was the subject of a public campaign against demolition in the 1970s when Devizes Council was considering building another inner relief road.

Originally two separate buildings, Nos 6 and 7 Monday Market Street were amalgamated into a single property surprisingly late in their lives by a householder

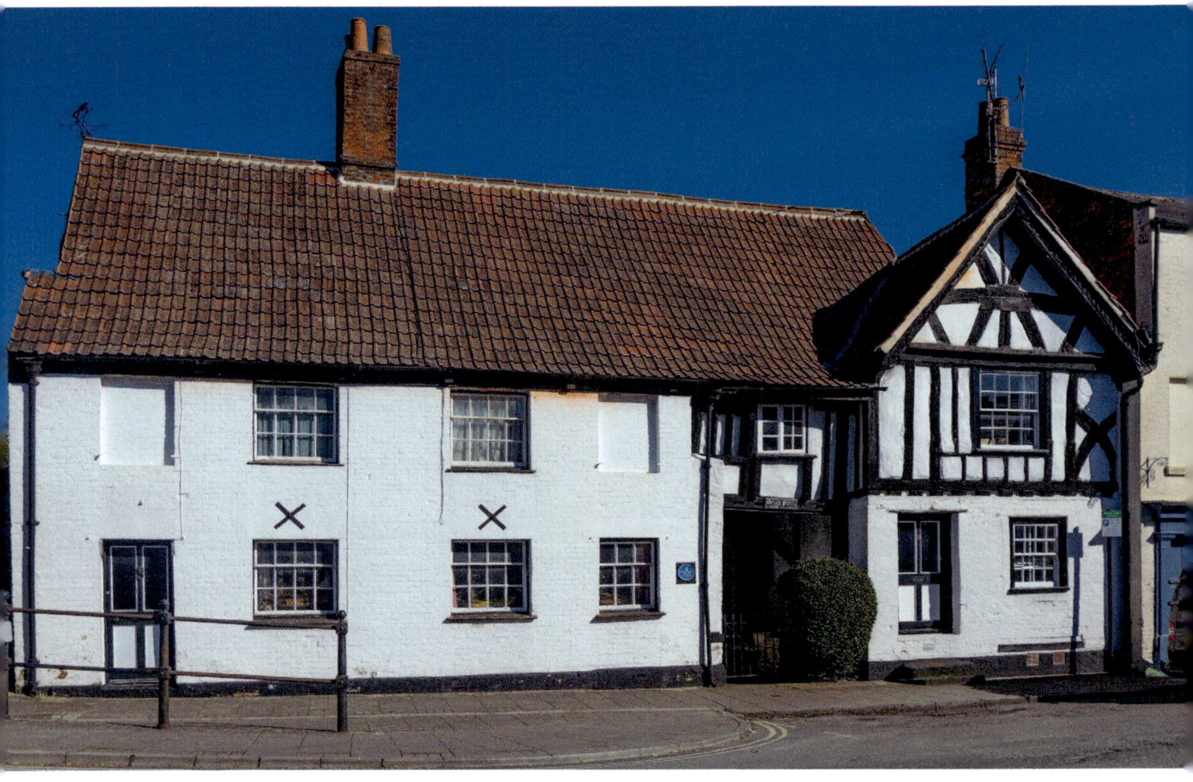

The Great Porch House, arguably the best-known historic building in Devizes.

whose daughter lived at No. 8. His restoration work included removing a large amount of later brick infill to allow the visible reopening of the imposing entrance and replacement of some later-style windows with those more suitable for the age of the building. While his work would be frowned upon today, it was admitted locally that his work brought the magnificence of the building back into the public eye and made a large contribution to the campaign to save it from demolition.

Great Porch House was constructed as a timber-framed, three-bay hall open from floor to roof with a two-storey cross-wing and a large porch or extended roofed section on the front. The latter, from which the building derived its name, was removed during the seventeenth century to allow for the construction of houses in the rear courtyard, called Great Porch Courtyard. This courtyard was originally framed by the two rear wings of the property, which were sadly demolished in 1954.

For anyone wishing to get a better idea of how the building looked originally with its porch intact, nearby Potterne has a medieval house with the exact same feature still in existence on the High Street.

The interior of Great Porch House sports two carved heads (the moulded wall joints join the intermediate trusses), those of King Henry IV and Queen Joan of Navarre, alongside a number of crude flower paintings in the roof. Likely originally the home of a rich merchant (the name of the Coventry family has been suggested), Queen Joan of Navarre is rumoured to have stayed here while repairs were being made to Devizes Castle. Now a private home, viewing of the interior is sadly no longer possible, but the finer points of it are well documented and a board is visible from the street that describes them for the curious.

The date board on the front of the building is charmingly decorated by tiny carved flowers beneath it – another sign of the expense incurred when the house was built. Few people could afford such unnecessary adornments on their buildings.

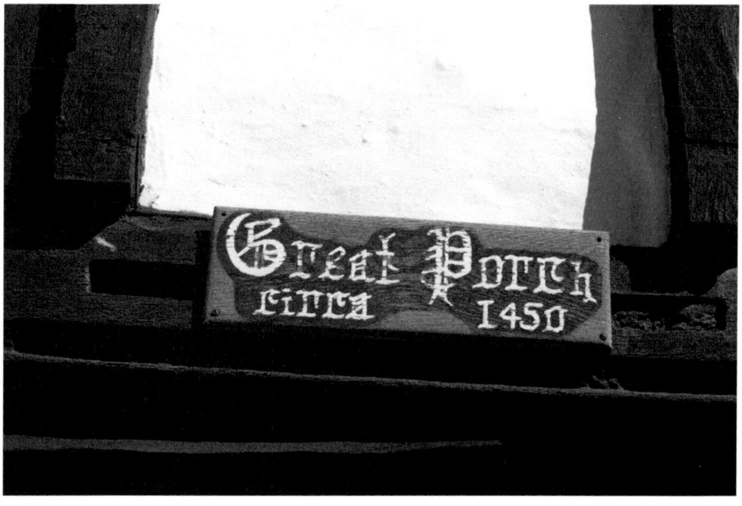

The Great Porch House nameplate.

The size and quality of finish to the original beams still visible above the entrance mark Great Porch House out as a very well-finished building and lend more evidence to the fact the family responsible for the original construction were very wealthy.

The original gable ends still remain in their original form. At the very rear of the house, though sadly not visible from the outside, is an original doorway. Some of the wattle-and-daub construction also remains visible within.

To quote the plaque, the Grand Porch House is 'an unusually good and most instructive town house of its type, as good as anything in England'. The building was given listed status in 1954.

Green

The green in Devizes is a large area of open grassland right in the centre of the town which is split in two by the A342. The two sections have become known locally as the 'large green' and 'small green' for obvious reasons.

The small green adjoins the Crammer and the Island and contains the children's play area, while the large green across the road offers a large, user-friendly and largely unspoilt open space which is much in demand during the summer for local events.

The small green adjoins the grounds of St James' Church to the north-east, whose churchyard dips down towards the waters of the Crammer, where a reinforcing wall was recently added to keep all safe and secure and to stop the churchyard slowly vanishing into the water.

The popular green at the centre of outdoor Devizes life.

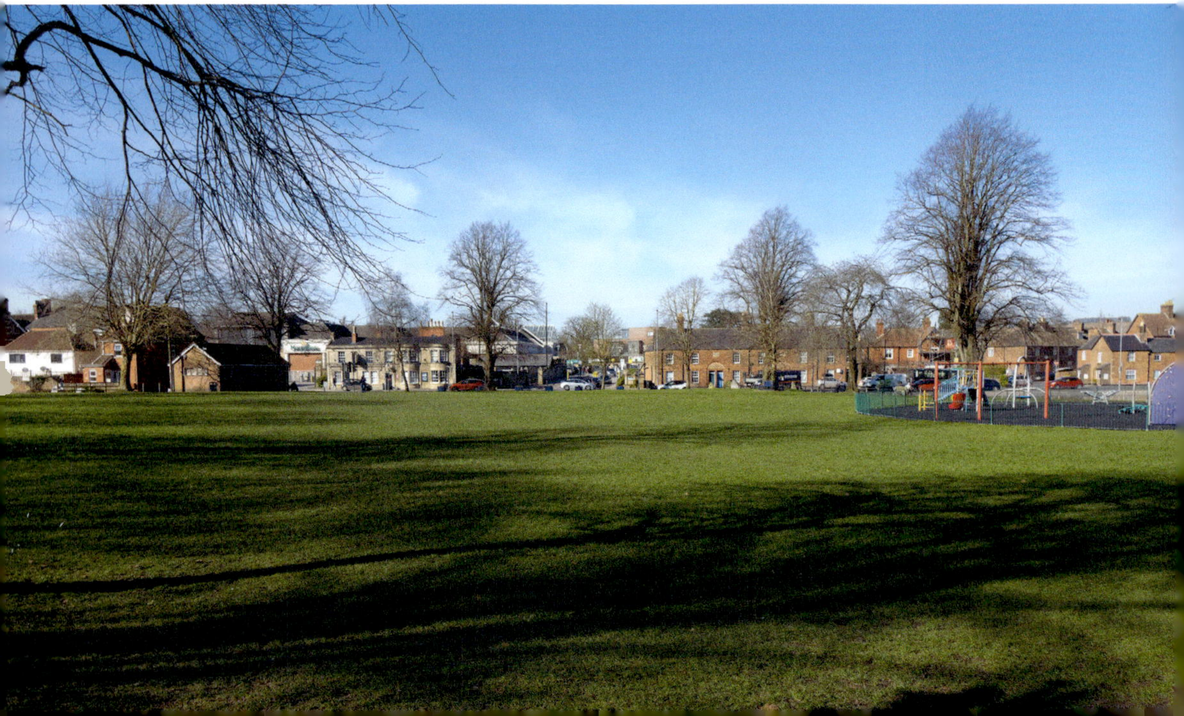

The large green remains largely free of additions and developments, and on a warm summer's day you will see the unspoilt greenery well used by locals as a space for relaxing while taking their lunch breaks or just reclining and taking in the glorious sunshine.

A wide range of feathered wildlife happily roams the green and Crammer when it is not in use for local events such as fairs, circuses and regular charity events. Due to local concerns for their welfare, the council website contains detailed information regarding what it is safe to feed them.

In the far corner of the green by the Crammer, you will see what initially appears to be a random arrangement of large stones. These are the 'twinning stones'. In a scheme started back 1951 by the Council of European Municipalities as a show of comradeship with Europe (and which later spread to other countries), towns were encouraged to forge links with specific towns in Europe by 'twinning' with them.

Dignitaries would visit each town and there would be ceremonies and presentations. At the height of this fashion, large numbers of families would enjoy reciprocal visits and long-standing and genuine friendships were often forged. Devizes became officially twinned with Mayenne in north-west France and Waiblingen in Germany.

To celebrate fifty years of the twinning, three stones – one from Devizes and one each from Mayenne and Waiblingen – were placed here on 24 June 2017.

The twinning stones on the green.

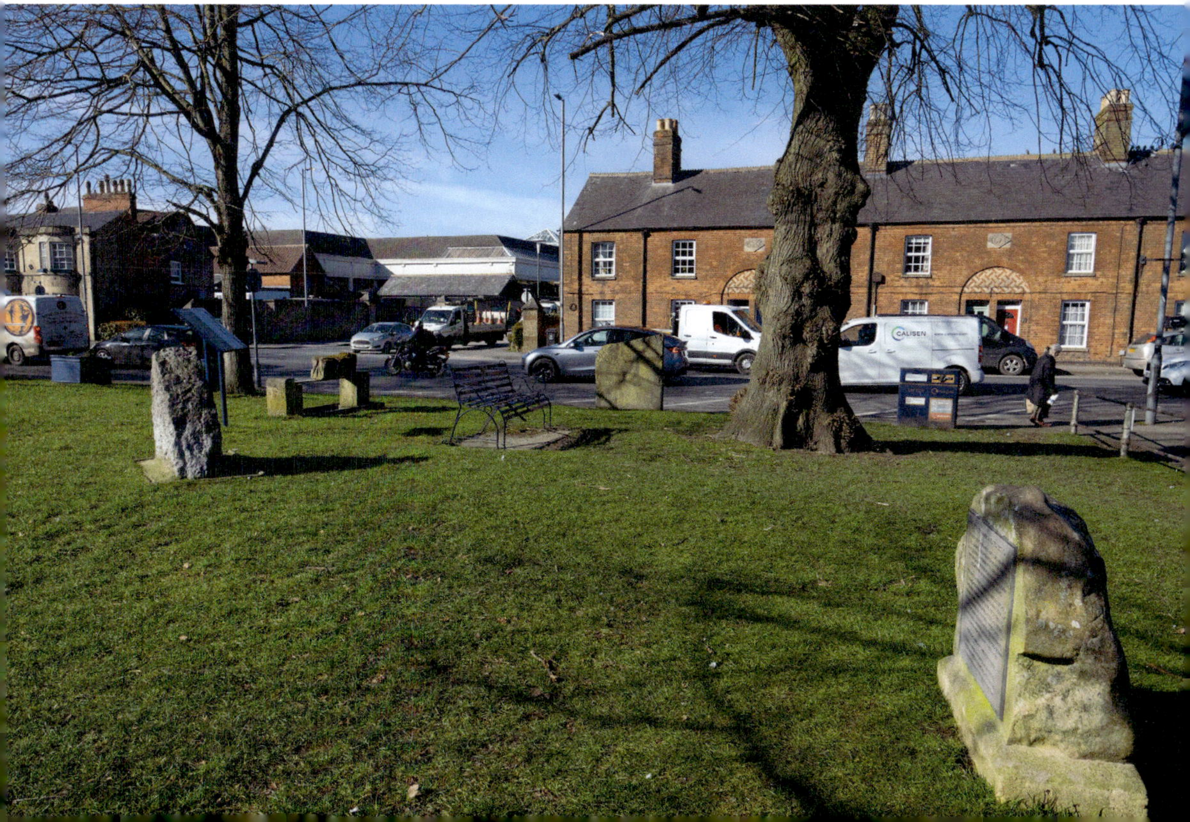

H

Handel House

Handel House is a square nineteenth-century building that stands on Sidmouth Street alongside the *Devizes Pyramid* and Albion Place. The name of the building appears on the front in black upcurving lettering, picked out by gold leaf above. The names of other composers are carved into the stonework around the top of the building below the eaves in a bold sans-serif font that is also picked out in gold leaf. There are Bach, Sullivan, Gluch, Spohr, Schuman, Mozart, Beethoven and Mendelssohn. The street-facing windows and the customer doors are framed by Greek-style columns supporting an entablature above them.

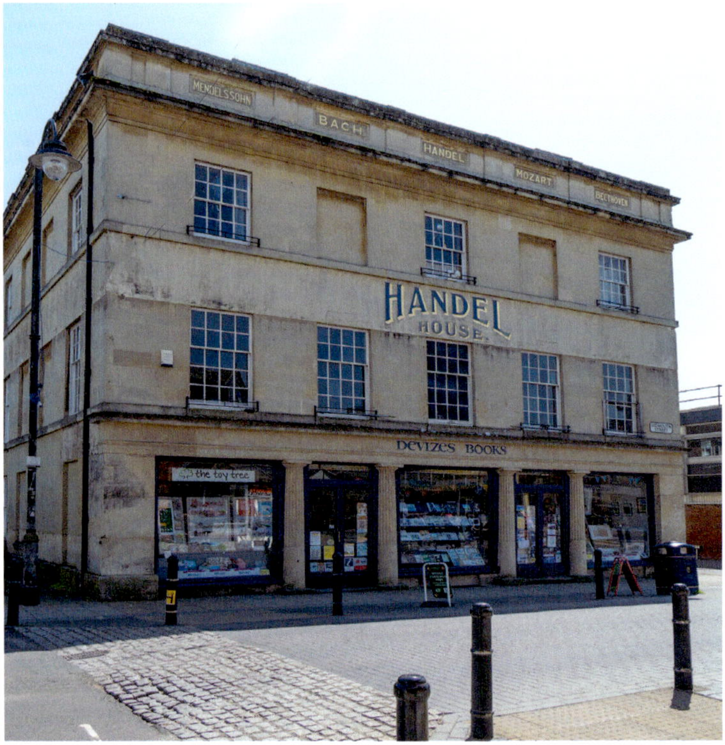

Handel House, once the home of musical retailer E. Price and Sons.

Handel House was the name given to all branches of the musical company E. Price and Sons. They were a supplier of musical instruments, gramophones and records, and were famous for having their own record label back in the days of 78-rpm records. According to customer reports, they were still selling a huge range of printed music that was still priced in old money well into the 1970s.

Founded by Ezra Price, a local man from West Lavington, this was the first Handel House and was created when they moved their piano and music showrooms from their original locations on Maryport Street and on the Brittox. Their second Handel House was on Princes Street in Yeovil, where Price's son lived and made his living manufacturing pianos. At their peak there were Handel Houses in Yeovil, Boscmbe, Winton, Southbourne, Bournemouth and Amesbury, listed as musical warehouses and musical instrument suppliers.

Ezra Price died in Handel House on 23 February 1904 at the age of seventy-nine. His business was passed on to his grandsons with an estate estimated at over **£7 million** in today's money. The business prospered for many more years, finally fading away in the late 1970s.

Currently, Handel House is the home of Devizes Books, and has been since 1981. A wide-ranging independent bookseller, they were voted 'Best Independent Shop' in the Devizes constituency in 2014 and are famous locally for their privately produced Devizes Walking Map, which places the town centrally with numerous walks radiating from it. They cheerfully claim to be able to get books from anywhere in the world and send them to anywhere else in the world. Most amusingly, they list one of their methods of ordering as 'notes shoved through the door', the first time this author has encountered such a method as an official policy. Their listed delivery methods include 'by dog walker if local'.

They are keen that their glorious building be preserved for future generations. Handel House was made a listed building in 1954.

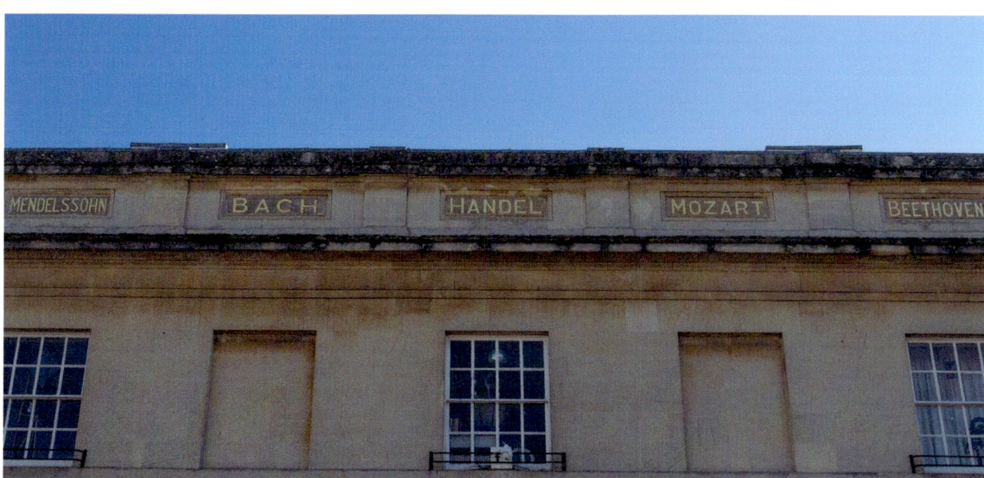

Famous composers are immortalised in gold leaf around the top of Handel House.

I

Island

The Island is a terraced group of timber-framed seventeenth-century cottages adjoining the green. Officially part of Nursteed Road, they have been listed buildings since September 1972. They have been built in two sections: one of plain red brick and the other a terrace in a classic two-storey design of rendered brickwork with unusual flush-mounted window frames. Each doorway has a classic triangular hood. The whole terrace is set well back from the main road and behind an unfenced garden which is traditionally a riot of flowers in spring and summer.

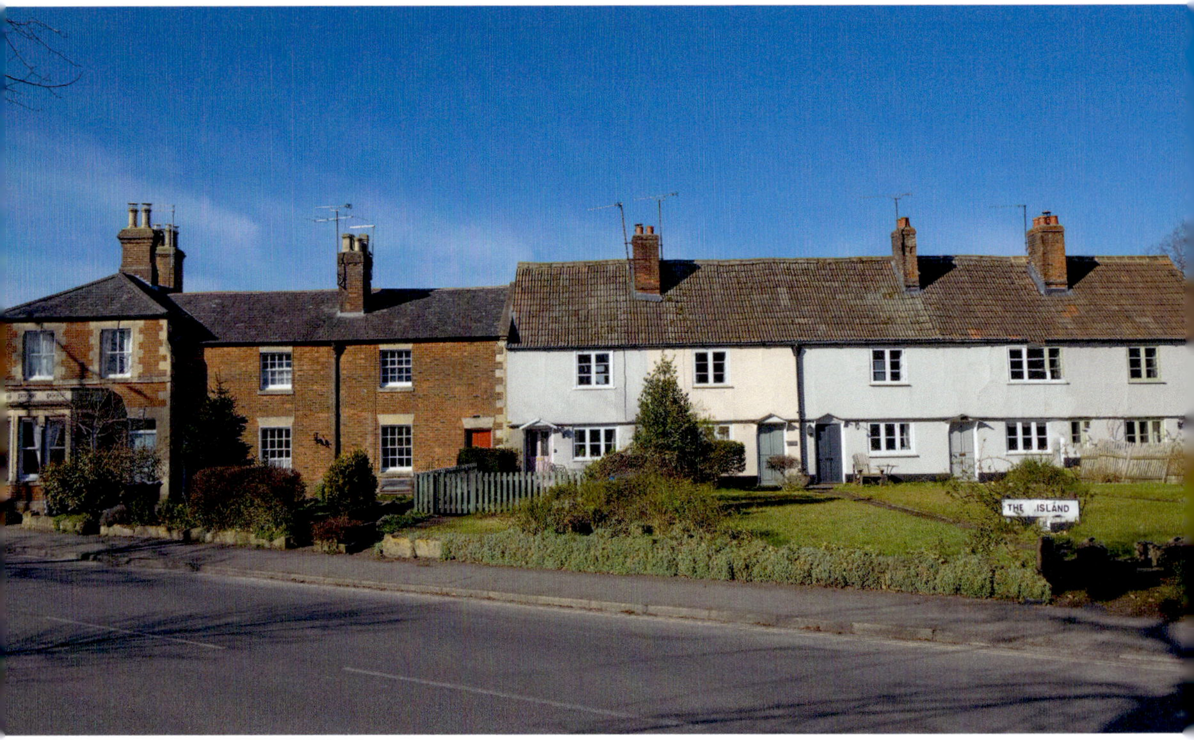

The Island by the green.

J

John Anstie

While being most famous for its corn markets and cloth production, Devizes once had a place in the now largely forgotten snuff trade.

Carrying a snuff box was once considered the mark of a gentlemen. People would be offered a 'pinch of snuff' in the same way it was once fashionable to offer round a cigarette case. Snuff itself is a very finely ground or pulverised form of tobacco, which was inserted (sniffed or snorted depending on whom you ask and which period is

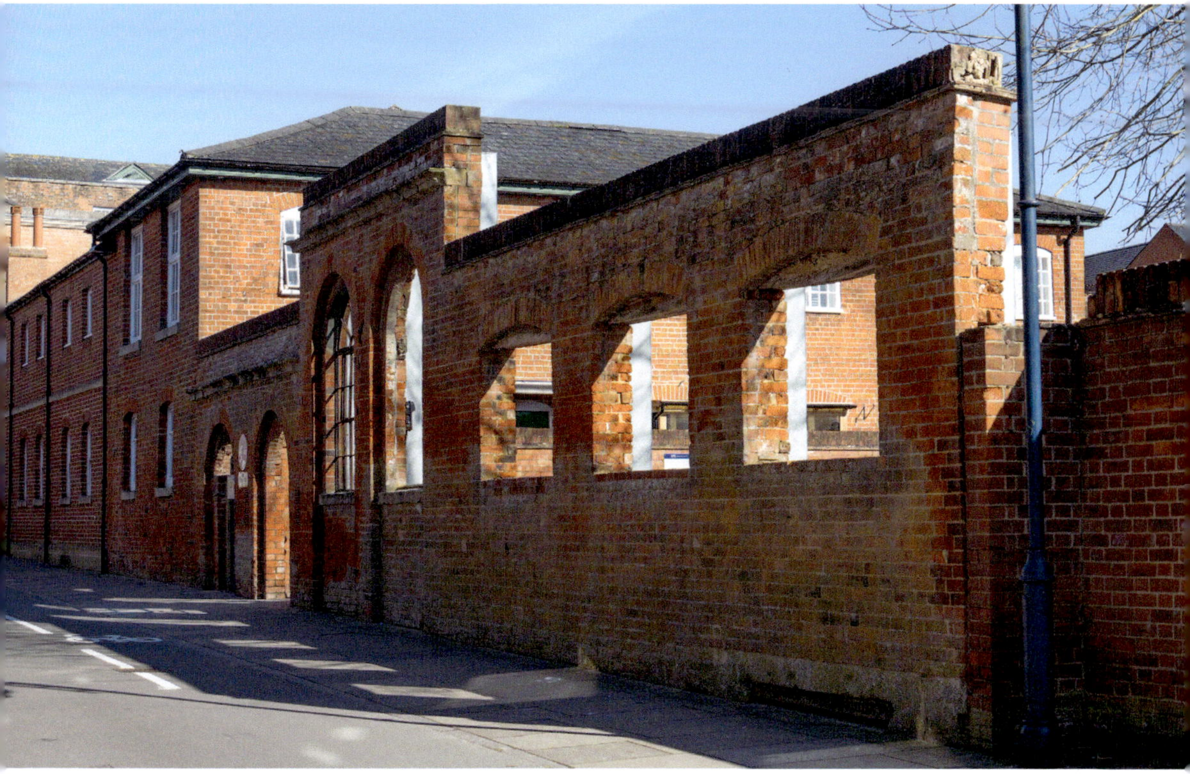

The remains of the snuff factory that gives Snuff Street its name.

being referred to) directly into the nostril to deliver both the nicotine and a floured scent at the same time. Traditionally, it was inhaled either from the back of the hand or directly from between the thumb and forefinger.

Devizes was once the location of Anstie's snuff and tobacco mill, located on New Street and Market Place. Over a period of time New Street became known as Snuff Street – the name it still bears today. This was the location of John Anstie's father's grocery business, which diversified into the supply of clothes, pepper, spices and tobacco. Seeing the rapidly increasing popularity of snuff, he chose to specialise in it and built a large snuff mill, the remains of which are still visible today. So successful was the snuff and tobacco trade that Anstie took two of his sons into the business as his partners. Famously, John Anstie carried his snuff in a gilt snuffbox with a Bromham quartz pebble inlaid on the lid, a reminder of where his family had first settled locally.

But John Anstie's snuff production did not last long. In 1784, he bought himself out of the business he owned with his sons for £500 and built a new factory at the opposite end of Snuff Street, at the junction with New Park Street, to embrace new methods of mass production in the cloth trade.

A grand building of pale brickwork, it reputedly towered above the surrounding timber buildings and was remarkable for the sheer number of windows it had (there are over 100), allowing good light for the cloth-production process. John Anstie is celebrated in the ornate and complex carving above the grand front door, where his

John Anstie's cloth factory on New Park Street.

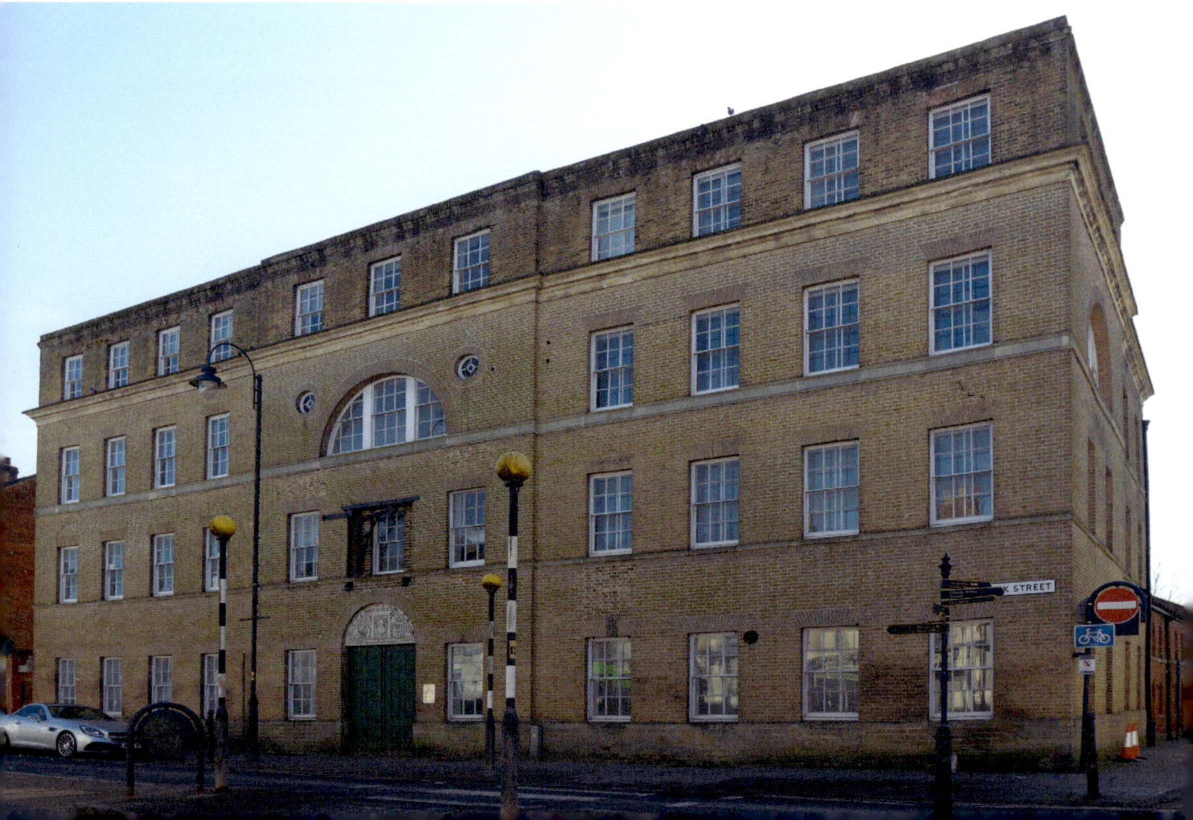

portrait and initials are surrounded by scenes of his modern weaving machinery, looms, traditional tools and the steps of cloth production, all below a design of the sheep that provided the wool. Today, a helpful key to what all the parts of the carving represent has been thoughtfully affixed to the wall alongside the door.

The interior of the building was described at the time as being well presented with oak beams and elm joists. Cranes for the loading and unloading of wagons are still visible to the side of the building, behind ornate iron gates and folded above the front door. This building was listed in 1954.

John Anstie was aware of riots by weavers in other towns when factories started to take over from home-based piecework. As such, he was known for his fairness. At one stage he was the local arbiter for disputes between weavers and factory workers brought before local Justices of the Peace. At the height of his business empire, he ran ten properties involved in the various processes that made up the complete process of cloth production.

John Anstie died in October 1830 in Bristol, where he was living in reduced circumstances brought about by his bankruptcy in December 1793, caused by changes in the weaving trade. He is buried in St Paul's Churchyard in Portland Square, Bristol. His brother, Benjamin, took over his mill at Poulshot, turning it into a mill for snuff grinding. The grand factory in Devizes was leased to the Devizes Overseers of the Poor as a house of industry.

The ornate display above the door of John Anstie's factory depicting the stages of cloth production.

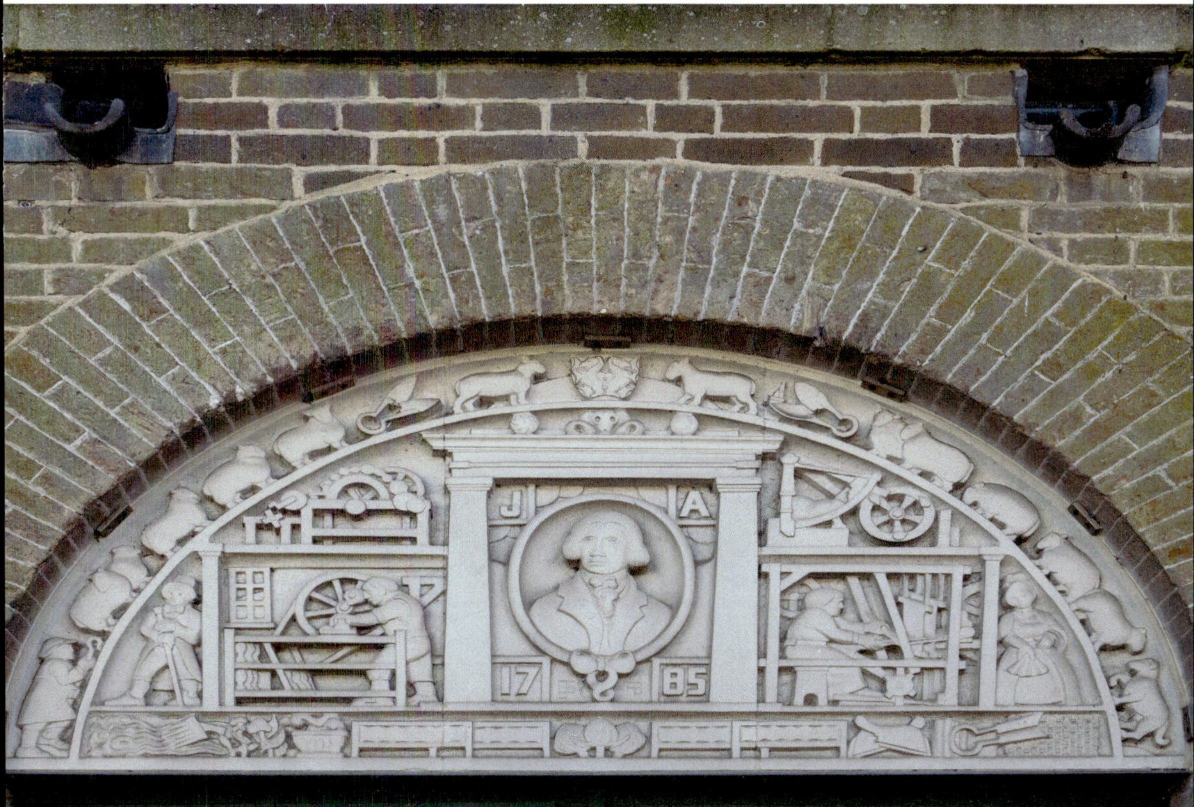

K

Kennet and Avon Canal

The Kennet and Avon Canal stretches 87 miles from the Bristol Channel to London. It features 104 locks along its length, including the twenty-nine that make up the Caen Hill Locks flight (see p. 11). The idea of the basic design and route of the canal can be traced back to Elizabethan times, when traders sought a way to avoid the treacherous passage through the English Channel in transporting their goods from western England to London.

The small boats of the time were prone to damage or loss from storms at sea, not to mention attack from French ships and pirates. At the time there was much discussion about the issue, but no action was taken. There was renewed interest following the upheaval of the English Civil War, but all attempts to get an Act through Parliament to make it a reality were defeated, largely by local landowners.

Plans to link the Kennet and Avon rivers had been hypothetically discussed for many years, but the work to make this a reality started after an Act of Parliament was finally passed in 1794 and a route was set through Devizes. The canal was completed in 1810 when the Caen flight of locks was finally completed. Originally named the Western Canal, the name was changed to the Kennet and Avon Canal to prevent confusion with the Grand Western Canal that was also under construction at the time.

Technically, the Kennet and Avon Canal is made up of three separate waterways: two navigable rivers linked by a stretch of man-made canal. The man-made section links the River Kennet at Newbury to the River Thames at Reading. Work on the River Kennet had made it navigable to shipping from Reading to Newbury in 1724, and to Bath by 1727. The Thames beyond Reading had been navigable for centuries.

Workings began at Bradford-on-Avon at the western end and at Newbury in the east. Ground was first broken at Bradford-on-Avon in October 1794. Through successful, traffic never reached the heights expected, and when the Great Western Railway opened their line over a broadly similar route in 1841 the canal went into decline. Income was reported to have quickly halved; as they began to make a loss, the canal was sold to the Great Western Railway with an intention on their part to turn it into a railway line. The Act of Parliament required that would allow this to happen was never passed, however, and the canal remained navigable and a working canal until 1948.

Plans to extend it to link up with the Basingstoke Canal were extensively discussed. A route was even surveyed in 1824, but these plans were never put into place.

During the early days of Second World War, when a German invasion of Great Britain seemed a real possibility, the Kennet and Avon Canal was part of the government's General Headquarters Line. This was a line of static structures intended to be used as defences to stop a German advance. Evidence of this defensive plan can still be seen in the form of hastily constructed pillboxes (small concrete defence points) at various points along the canal.

During the 1960s the canal fell into a serious decline and parts of it became no longer navigable. Work by the Kennet and Avon Canal Trust, a charity formed in 1962, saw the canal brought back into service as a fully navigable waterway over thirty years. It was officially reopened by Elizabeth II in August 1990.

Today the canal is a vibrant waterway, with a steady traffic of pleasure boats to enjoy the challenges of the locks and the glorious scenery. At first light every year on Good Friday, the Devizes to Westminster International Canoe Marathon gets underway. Contestants have to navigate all the locks involved; the average time taken is usually just over seventeen hours.

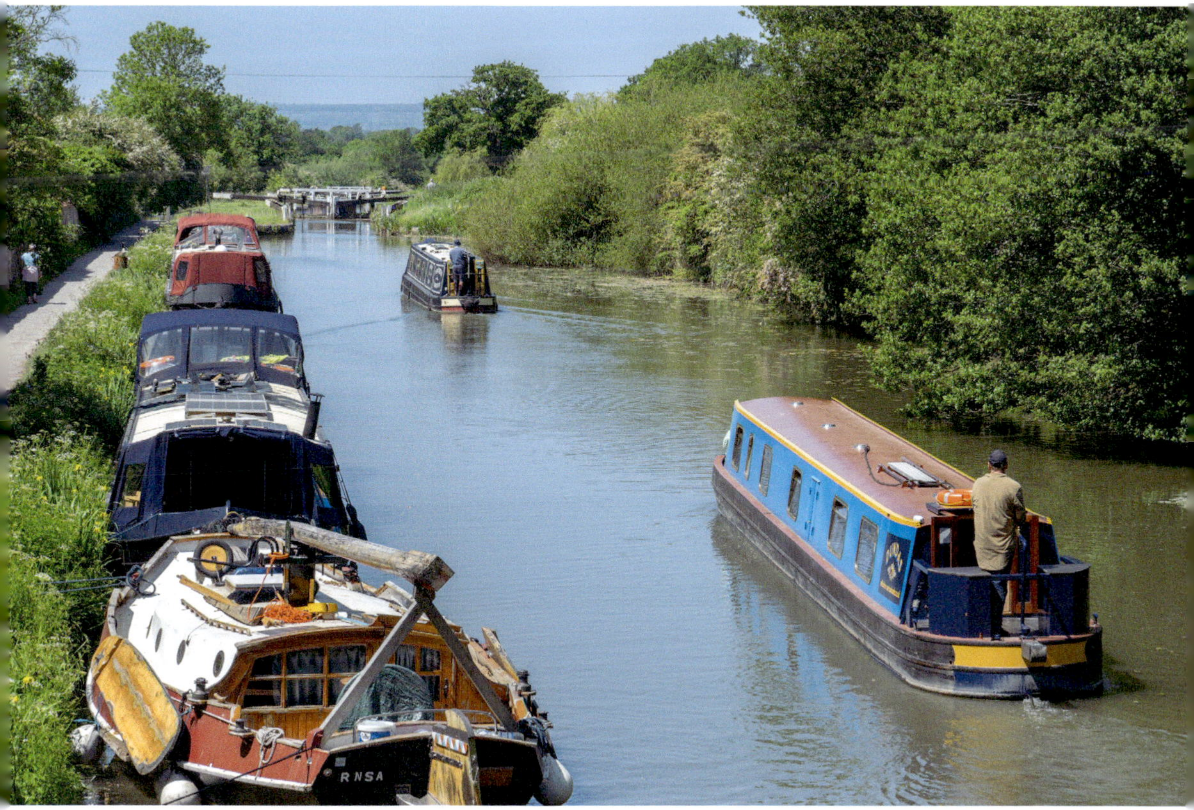

The Kennet and Avon Canal.

L

Le Marchant Barracks

As you travel north out of Devizes on London Road you will pass a large red-brick building. It is intricately detailed with limestone, local stone dressing and ornamentation with two huge square turrets at one end. This is the former Le Marchant Barracks.

Built in 1878 in a Gothic Revival style, it was designed by Major H. C. Sedden of the Royal Engineers as part of the Cardwell Reforms. It was named after Sir John Gaspard Le Marchant, Commanding Officer of the 99th Regiment. It was designed to be a self-contained barracks with permanent housing for 250 soldiers, including married quarters, over four floors. It even had its own cricket ground and large double doors to the rear of the building once housed their own fire engine.

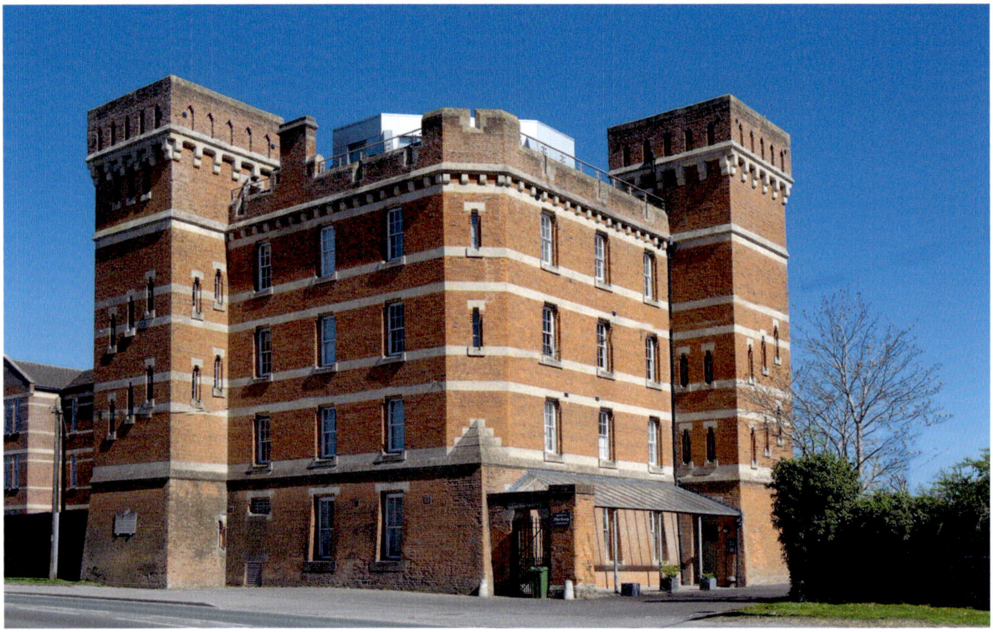

Le Marchant Barracks on London Road.

The Cardwell Reforms were a wide-ranging reorganisation of the British military system which 'localised' many regiments of the British army, adding locations to their regimental titles with the intention of attracting men from specific areas to their local regiments. At the time of construction, the barracks were home to the 62nd (Wiltshire) Regiment of Foot and the 99th (Lanarkshire) Regiment. These were amalgamated in 1881 into the Wiltshire (Duke of Edinburgh's) Regiment. Le Marchant Barracks remained their home depot through both World Wars until 1959. It then became the regimental museum (now moved to Salisbury) and remained a satellite depot to the Duke of Edinburgh's Royal Regiment until 1967.

During the First World War the barracks were used as the local infantry training school. Over 5,000 fresh recruits passed through the doors, alongside 3,000 reservists called back to the flag.

During the Second World War part of the barracks was used as a prisoner-of-war camp. By the end of 1944, 7,500 German prisoners were being held there following the successes of the Allied landing at D-Day.

In December 1944, the massed prisoners, under Waffen SS officers, planned what has become known as the Devizes Plot. Assuming there would be fewer guards at Christmas and that those who were there would be more interested in the festivities than their duties, the prisoners planned to break out of the camp and seize nearby RAF Yatesbury. Here, they would take control of weaponry, aircraft and armoured vehicles before, depending on whose account is considered accurate, they intended to attack London or make their way to the East Anglian coast in the hope of rescue by German forces from mainland Europe.

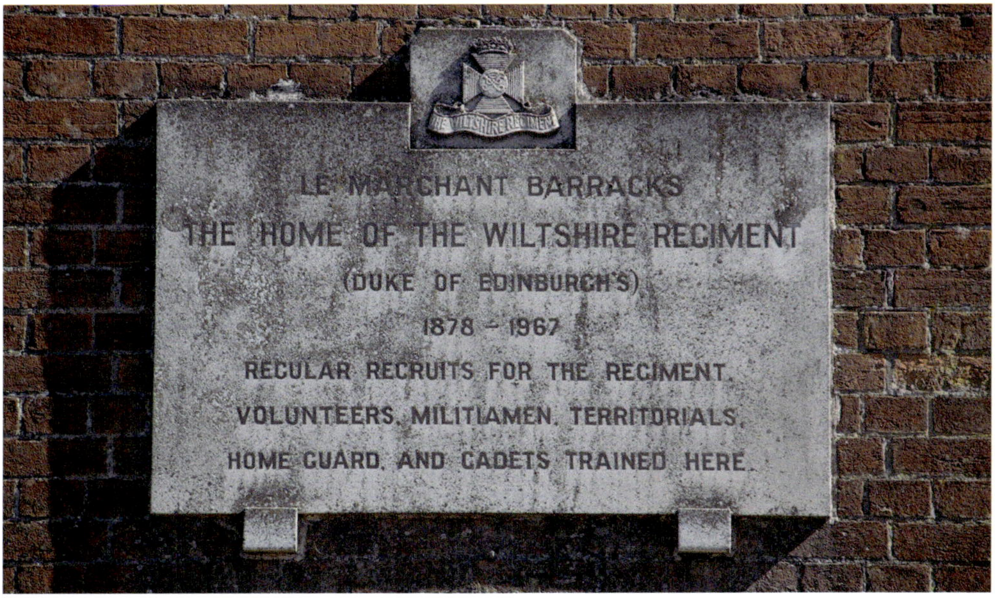

The Wiltshire Regiment commemorative plaque on Le Marchant Barracks.

The fact that RAF Yatesbury was a wireless training establishment and flying school with little more power than Tiger Moth biplanes to their name calls into question how well this plan would have succeeded, but a chance remark to an American interpreter put the British military on guard and the mass escape was prevented.

After 1967 part of the barracks remained in use as the home of the Territorial Army 1st Battalion, the Wessex Regiment, until the building was sold by the Ministry of Defence in the 1980s for housing and commercial use. At one stage a sizeable part was taken up by a war game store called Keep Wargaming. They still exist in Devizes and have retained an image of the barracks' famous tower as their logo. The barracks itself had become an entirely residential property by 2013.

As part of the Cardwell Reforms to make army recruitment more localised, these local barracks were listed as an important building in 1984. It is one of just ten remaining examples of these once numerous local barracks still in existence. The one in Reading very much resembles a smaller version of this one.

Leipzig Plantation

Overlooking Devizes from the north is the unusually named Leipzig Plantation. Consisting largely of beech trees and covering an area of over 4 hectares, it is a popular local dog-walking spot. There is also a free car park that offers access to the Devizes Millennium White Horse and other footpaths.

The Leipzig Plantation north of Devizes.

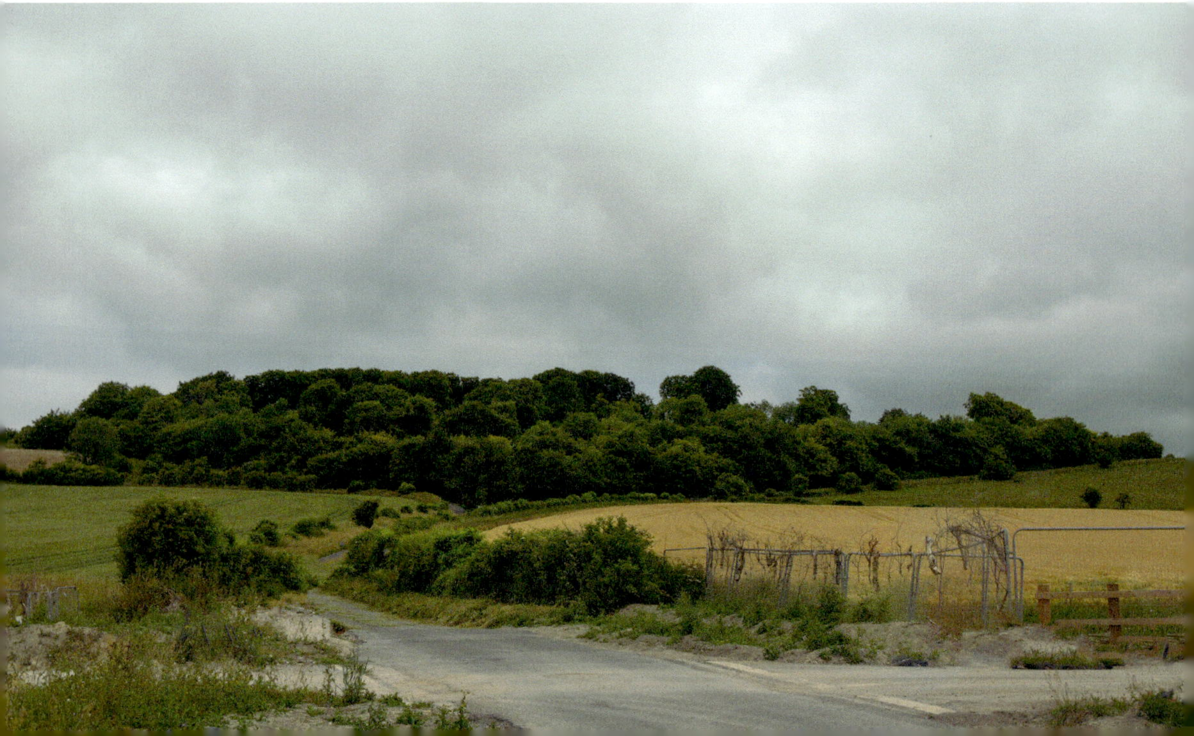

Some sources state the plantation was created in 1813 in commemoration of the Battle of Leipzig, while others claim it was planted much later during the Victorian era.

The Battle of Leipzig was fought on 16–19 October 1813 between the Napoleonic French army and the combined forces of the rest of mainland Europe, notably Austria, Prussia, Russia and Sweden under the command of Tsar Alexander I and Karl Von Schwarzenberg. The battle is also known as the Battle of Nations due to the huge number (for the time) of troops taking part. There were 200,000 under French command and 400,000 on the side of the allies. The battle was a decisive victory for the coalition forces against the French, and Napoleon was forced to retreat to France and put an end to his dreams of conquering the whole of Europe. It was the largest battle fought on mainland Europe until the horrors of the First World War a century later.

The plantation stands at an unusual point where the catchment area of three rivers meet. Rain falling on the plantation runs off in three distinct direction, towards the three separate rivers – the Bristol Avon to the west, the Kennet to the east and the Salisbury Avon to the south.

M

Market Cross

Dominating the centre of the Market Place in Devizes, through which all main roads pass, is the magnificent Gothic Market Cross. Constructed on the site of the original Market Cross, the current one was completed in 1814. It was built to the design of architects James and Benjamin Wyatt, a father and son team. James sadly died in a coach accident before he could witness the completion of the project.

The design was financed by Henry Addington, Viscount Sidmouth, who had been the MP for Devizes between 1784 and 1805, rising to the rank of Home Secretary and then on to the position of prime minister before finally being elevated to the House of Lords. A bronze plaque commemorating his contribution is affixed to one face of the structure.

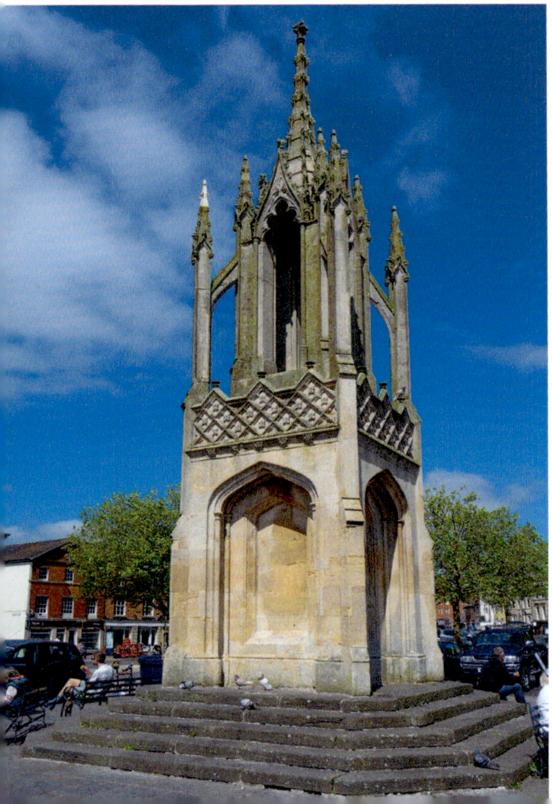

The Market Cross.

The Market Cross is a tall structure standing on a five-stepped, paved, octagonal plinth, above which are sculpted arches on all four sides. Flying buttresses support a tall and extensively decorated centre pinnacle with carved decorations in a poppy motif. Bronze plaques on the main body tell the story of Ruth Pierce (see p. 66).

The markets commemorated by the Market Cross have been held in the Market Place on a Thursday since the town received it's market charter, all the way back in the 1141. The charter was granted by Empress Matilda in gratitude to the people of Devizes who laid siege to the castle on her behalf and handed it to her upon its surrender. She made Devizes a borough under Crown law, a status that would continue until a Parliamentary reshuffle in 1974. The market is considered to be one of the longest continuously running markets in the UK.

The first officially recorded market in Devizes was in 1228, although by this time it is believed to have been running unrecorded for many years. It grew steadily through the centuries and by the eighteenth century it was considered to be the largest corn market in the West Country. Other products, such as hops, cattle, horses and cloth, were also well represented at these markets.

Today, much of the open space that would once have been taken up with produce market stalls is given over to car parking most of the time; however, to this day, every Thursday it is given over to market stalls selling local goods and fresh produce, and many locals will tell you it is still the best market for these in the area. Long may this tradition continue.

The Market Cross was made a listed building in 1954.

Millennium White Horse

Officially known as the Devizes Millennium White Horse and sometimes referred to as the 'Roundway Down White Horse', this chalk figure looks down on Devizes from the north, from above the village of Roundway.

There were originally eight examples of white horses cut into the hills in this area, with one more on the west side of Roundway that was considered lost in 1922 with no surviving sketches or notes of the size or shape. James Smith, head boy of Devizes Grammar School, was cycling the area and noted discolouration in the grass on the west of Roundway Down in 1954 visible under certain lighting conditions. He sketched out what he believed was the shape of the lost white horse of Devizes (sometimes known as 'Snobs Horse' after the shoemakers who had originally created it – 'snobs' being a local term for shoemakers). The outline has been periodically seen since and regularly makes the local news, but attempts to resurrect it have always failed. Smith drew a sketch of what he could make out of the horse, and it is from his work that the rough design of the new white horse was derived.

Seeking an unusual way to mark the dawning of the new millennium in 2000, Devizes resident Sarah Padwick sent a letter to the local paper in 1998 suggesting an

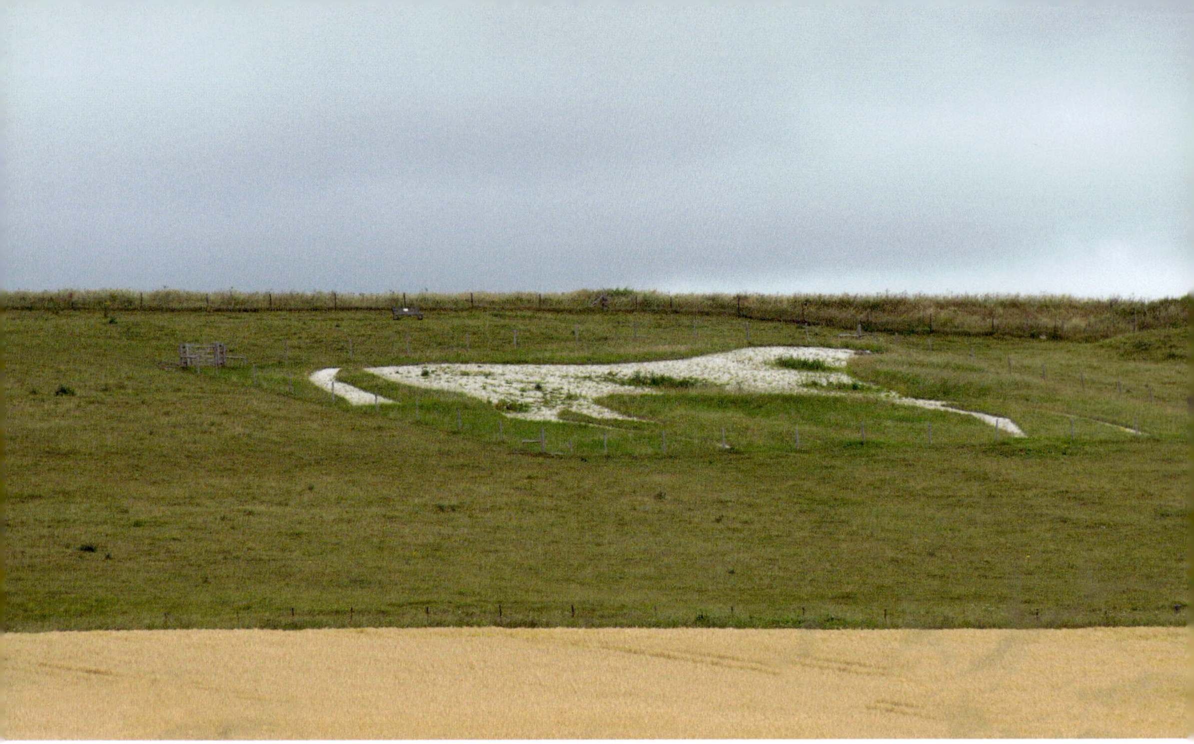

Devizes Millennium White Horse.

excellent way to mark its arrival would be by cutting a new white horse into the chalk overlooking the town. An attempt in the same year to resurrect the original 'Snobs Horse' failed due to the rules regarding the site being an Area of Special Scientific Interest.

Local farmer Chris Combe offered one of his fields as a site for the proposed new horse. The Crown Estates Commissioners, who owned the land, approved the use and the sketch made by James Smith was used as the inspiration for the design of the new horse. The new design by Peter Trevor Greed was reversed to face to the right, one of only four in the UK to do so, rather than to the left as the original had. And unlike every other white horse in Wiltshire, it was depicted as moving rather than standing still.

The rather grandly named Cavaliers of the Devizes White Horse Committee was established to oversee the project. Local company Pearce Civil Engineering provided the heavy equipment required for ground clearing and placing the large stones needed to mark the eye and nostril of the horse.

The horse was cut into the chalk on the weekend of 18 and 19 September 1999, with over 200 volunteers involved with the groundwork. The final figure lies nearly 230 metres long and was finally considered complete on 29 September 1999.

Known locally as 'Chalkie' and kept clean and clear though the efforts of the community service group of the probation service, the new white horse has been adopted as the symbol of the Roundway Parish Council and Nursteed Community Primary School in Devizes. The latter, on the tenth anniversary of the completion of the figure, created a one-tenth scale version on the school grounds which is still there today.

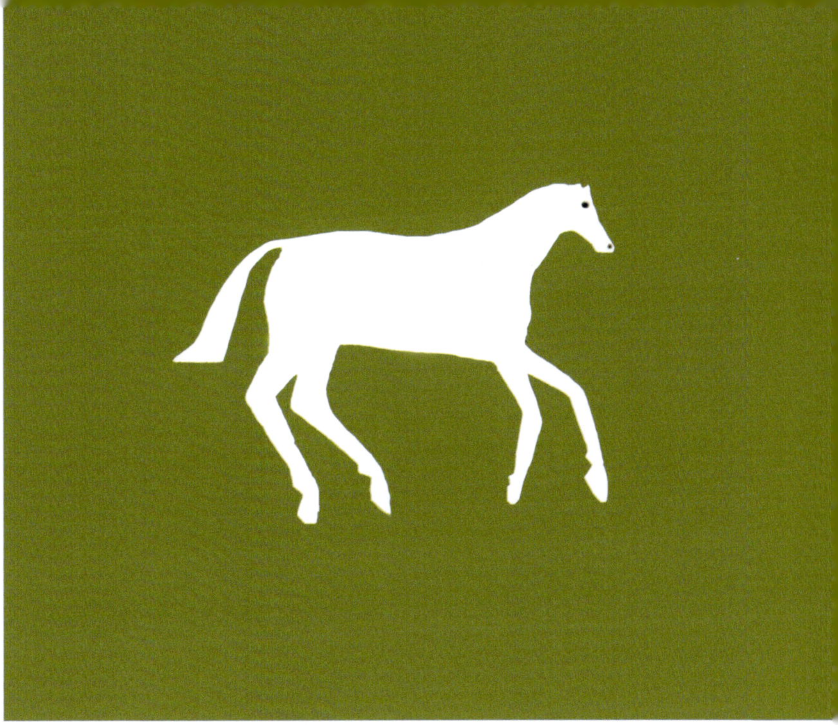

A sketch showing the exact shape of the Devizes Millennium White Horse.

'Chalkie' has also been added to the Wiltshire White Horse Walking Trail, a 90-mile-long trail that takes in all the existing Wiltshire white horses for those of a very physically active disposition.

Monday Market Street

For more years than most care to recall, Thursday has been market day in Devizes; certainly, it is listed as such in every venerable guidebook the author has to hand. Several sources list this as being the case for at least the last 300 years, possibly since the town received its royal charter from Empress Matilda in 1141.

Before this Thursday tradition took hold, Devizes was most unusual in having two market days and technically in different parishes. The Monday market, commemorated by Monday Market Street, took place in St Mary's, while the still-existing Thursday market took place in the parish of St John's.

Monday Market Street has now been encroached upon by many buildings, but the name remains as a memory of what came before. With the Great Porch House at one end and many handsome eighteenth-century buildings scattered among the more modern properties, a background in trade is clear. A number of the older buildings have bricked-over access ways or they have been converted to balconies on their first floors, where loading and unloading winches once operated. Many newly converted properties are still fronted by fine Georgian doorways.

Now occupied by a fish and chip shop, No. 13 is a particularly fine building with a grand cornice and pediment, flanked on one side by a window clearly showing a thick stone construction beam above.

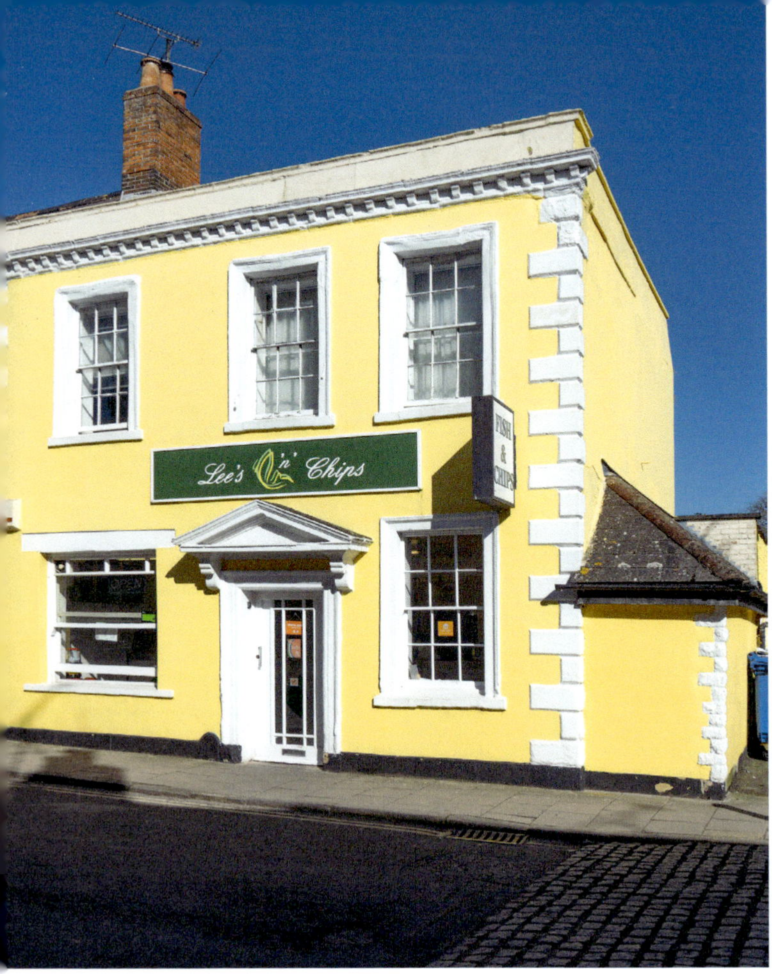

Left: No. 13 Monday Market Street has fine architectural features, including a large pediment over the door.

Below: The commercial origins of many buildings on Monday Market Street are clear.

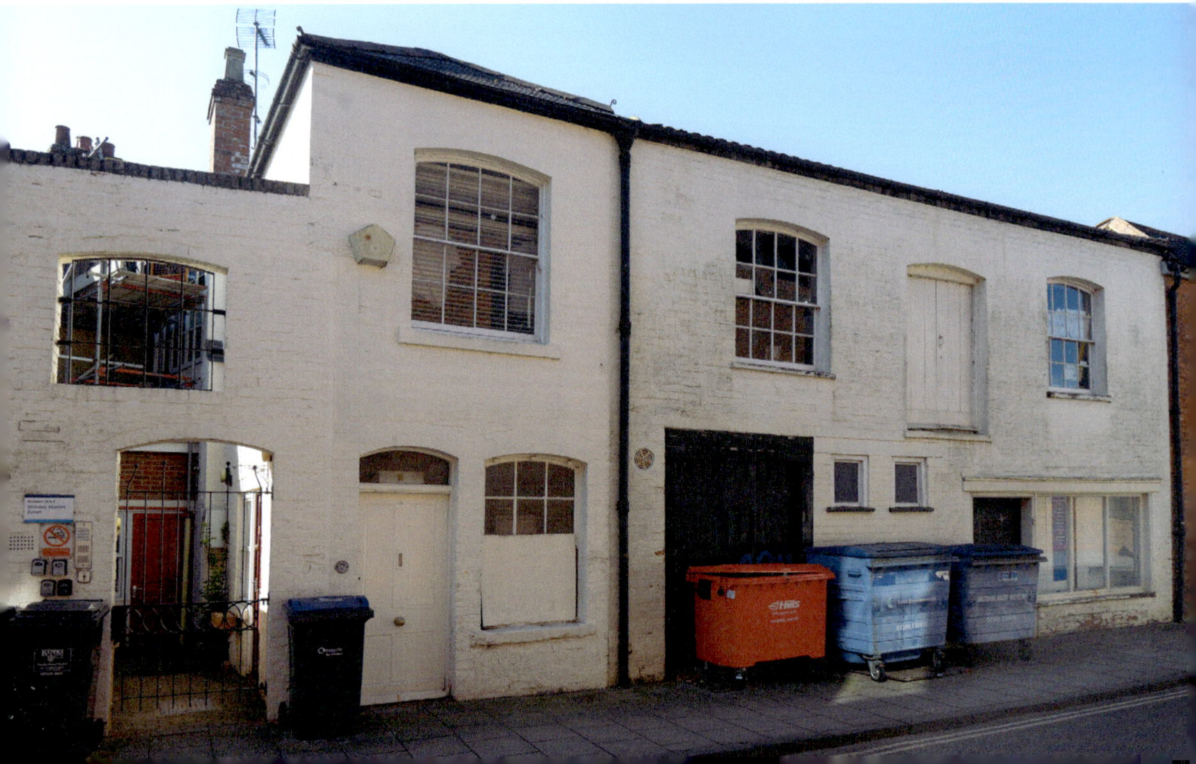

N

Norman Castle

The castle that Devizes was formed around dates back to Norman times, and the Victorian castle that stands in the centre of the town today is on largely the same spot as the original. The town was originally known in Latin as Castrum ad Divisas, or 'Castle at the Boundaries', as it stood at the point at which three ancient parishes met. While some early maps spell the name of the town 'Devyses', the last part of the Latin name was eventually corrupted into the name we have today, Devizes.

The original wooden Norman motte-and-bailey castle is believed to have been built around 1080 by Osmund, Bishop of Salisbury, on the site of an even older Iron Age fortress. Later archaeology has found that the ditch was 4.5 metres deep and around 8 metres wide.

Though not mentioned in the Domesday Book of 1086, there is a record of the castle as early as 1106 when it was documented that Robert of Normandy was imprisoned there for twenty years by his brother King Henry I.

The original wooden structure is said to have burned down in 1113 and was rebuilt, this time in stone, by Roger le Poer, the new Bishop of Salisbury. King Stephen of England claimed and occupied the castle during the 1130s, followed by Empress Matilda, who took control when the locals stormed it on her behalf. She in turn returned it to King Stephen before taking control of it again soon after. One twelfth-century observer described Devizes Castle as being the 'finest castle in Europe', by which time it also featured a large, enclosed deer park on the western approach.

Officially a Crown property, the castle was used as a prison by Henry II and Henry III before Henry VIII gave the castle to his first wife, Catherine of Aragon, before reclaiming it for the Crown after their divorce.

During the English Civil War, Royalist forces garrisoned the castle and were besieged by Parliamentarian forces under Sir William Waller prior to the Battle of Roundway Down, at which the Royalists were victorious. After this, both the castle and Devizes remained under the command of Sir Charles Lloyd, chief engineer of King Charles I.

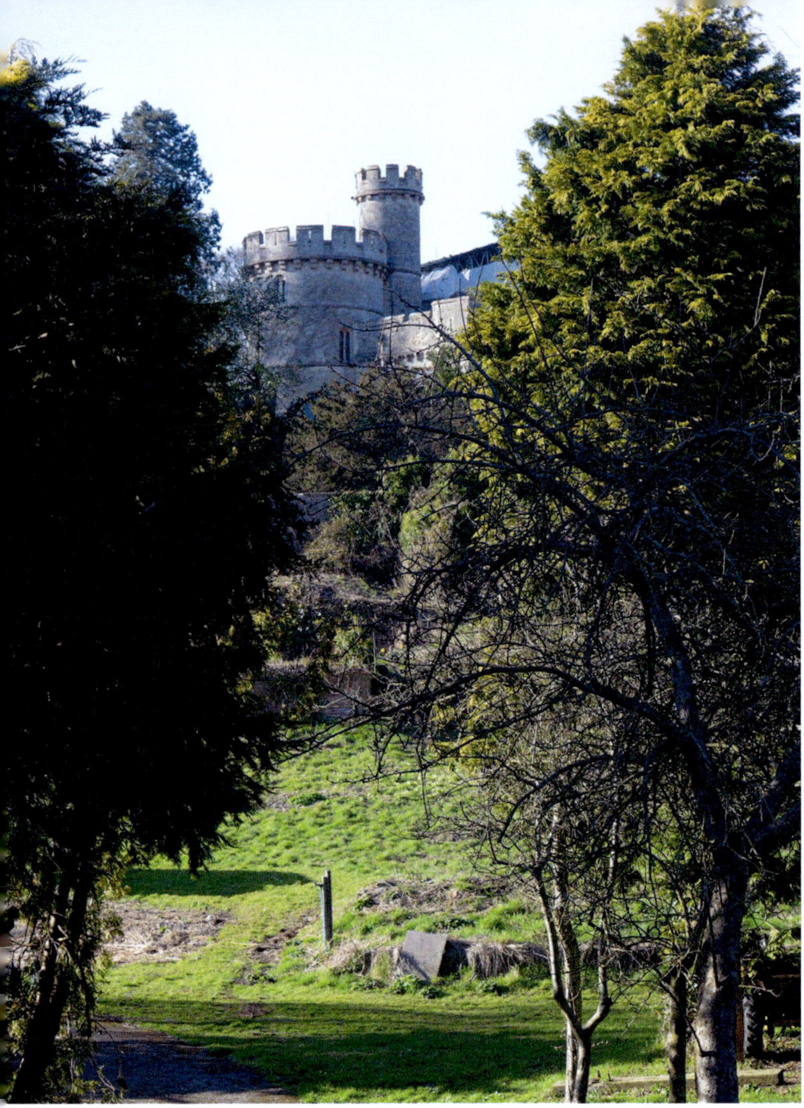

The turrets of the private home that is now considered Devizes Castle.

In September 1645, the revolutionary Parliamentarian New Model Army under Oliver Cromwell besieged the castle with a strong force of over 5,000 men and artillery. The garrison surrendered following a bombardment.

After the Civil War, the castle was demolished (in a process known at the time as slighting) in 1648 and the stone was used for local building projects. All that remained after the slighting was the original mound, the remains of the moat and some scattered foundations that are all still visible today.

In 1838, the land and remains of the castle were acquired by Valentine Leach, a local businessman who set about building a Victorian interpretation of the castle, much like the Victorian interpretation of the Roman baths that exist nearby in Bath. Less kind sources described the new building as a Gothic Revival fantasy castle.

Prolific architect Henry Edmund Goodridge of Bath produced a castellated design in a mixture of Gothic Revival and romanticised Norman design styles, construction

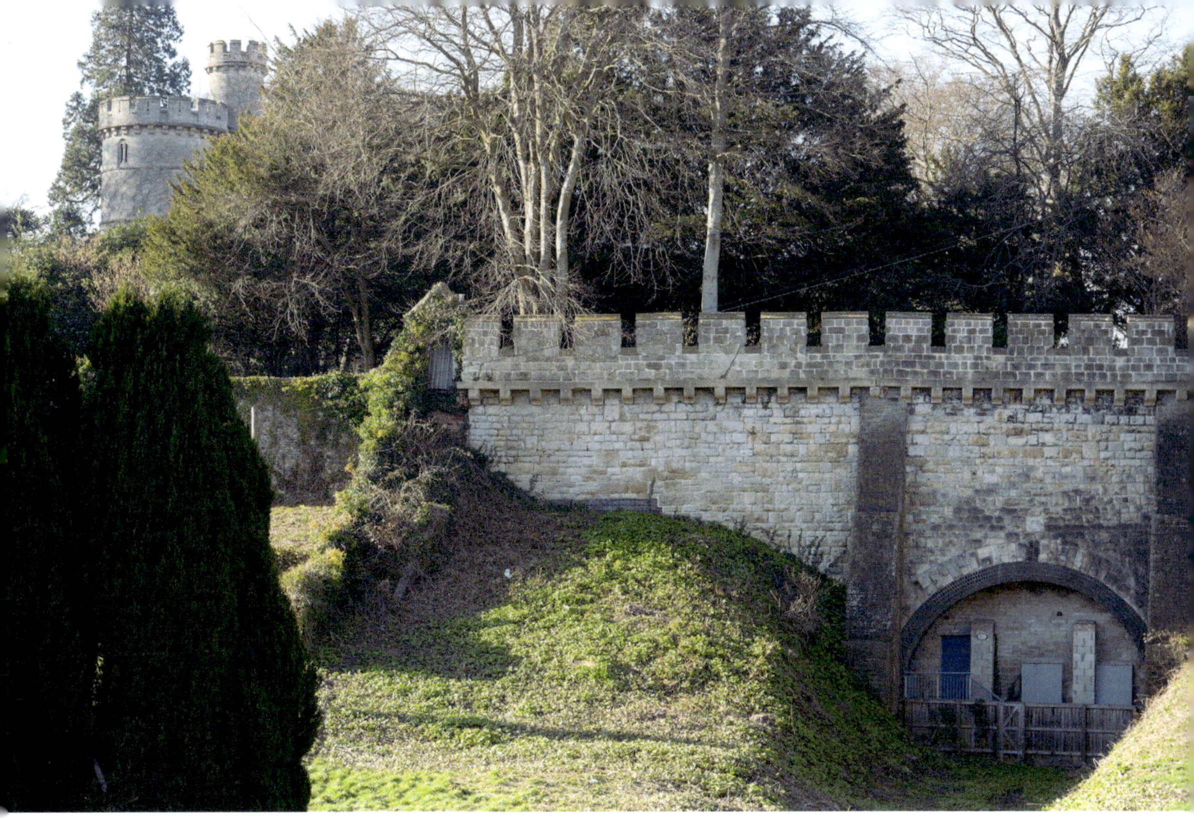

The lower levels of Devizes Castle reveal its earlier origins.

of which began in 1842. It continued to grow over the following decades into a large, modern house and was later split into two homes: North and South Tower.

When the large home now known as the South Tower (which had been the main part of the castle) was listed for sale in 2019, it was described as standing on a 2.4-acre plot and having an area of 9,117 square feet. There were said to be eight bedrooms, six bathrooms and press releases spoke of living spaces spread over four floors and an apartment in a turret. *Country Life* magazine described as 'suitable for sleeping beauty' and it has reputedly been described as 'the most beautiful castle in Christendom'.

The much smaller North Tower structure is based on a seventeenth-century windmill. It is believed that the rubble base upon which it stands is of material from the original castle. The terrace that surrounds the site still retains a section of rare, original Norman-era stonework bearing a zigzag pattern.

Examining the castle site today on a street map, it is clear that the town grew up around it. The streets are arrayed around the original castle site and its lines of defence. A very similar pattern can be seen in the road plan of Salisbury, leading experts to theorise that the Bishops of Salisbury, the original architects of the castle, were instrumental in the growth plans of both towns.

During the Second World War, the castle was used to house Italian prisoners of war. Today it remains a magnificent private home with views both out over the downs and over Devizes itself.

The castle as it stands was made a listed building in September 1972.

O

Oddfellows Hall

If you look up while wandering along Maryport Street, beneath three grand arched windows and above two large brick arches, you will see an unusual and seldom noticed war memorial on the front of Oddfellows Hall. It lists the members of this branch of the Oddfellows Society who fell in the First World War. Despite the official cessation of hostilities at eleven o'clock on 11 November 1918, the fighting sadly did not stop then and conflicts continued until well into 1919, and arguably even later.

The Oddfellows Society is a friendly society founded in 1810 which exists to this day. It is a society that promotes friendship, charitable works and enables people to enjoy a better social life while not having any specific religious affiliations.

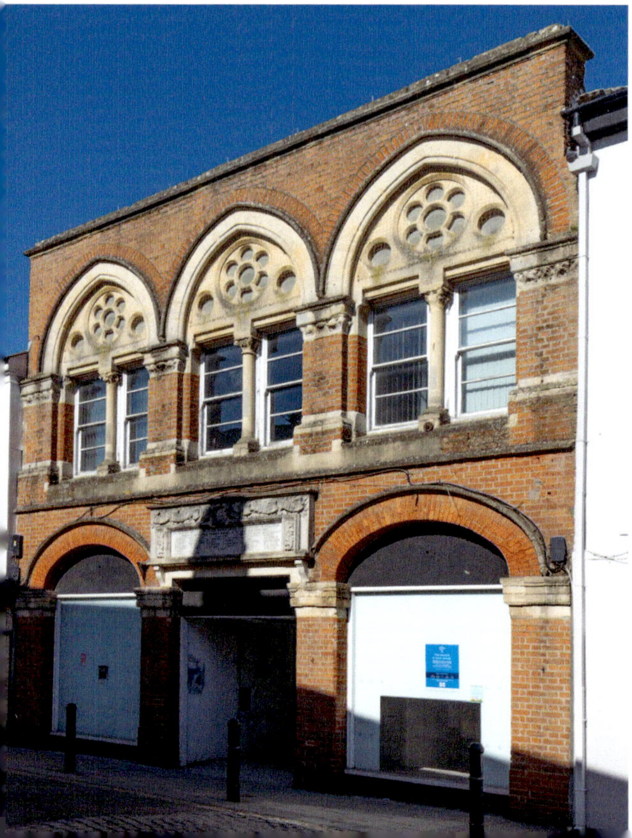

Oddfellows Hall on Maryport Street.

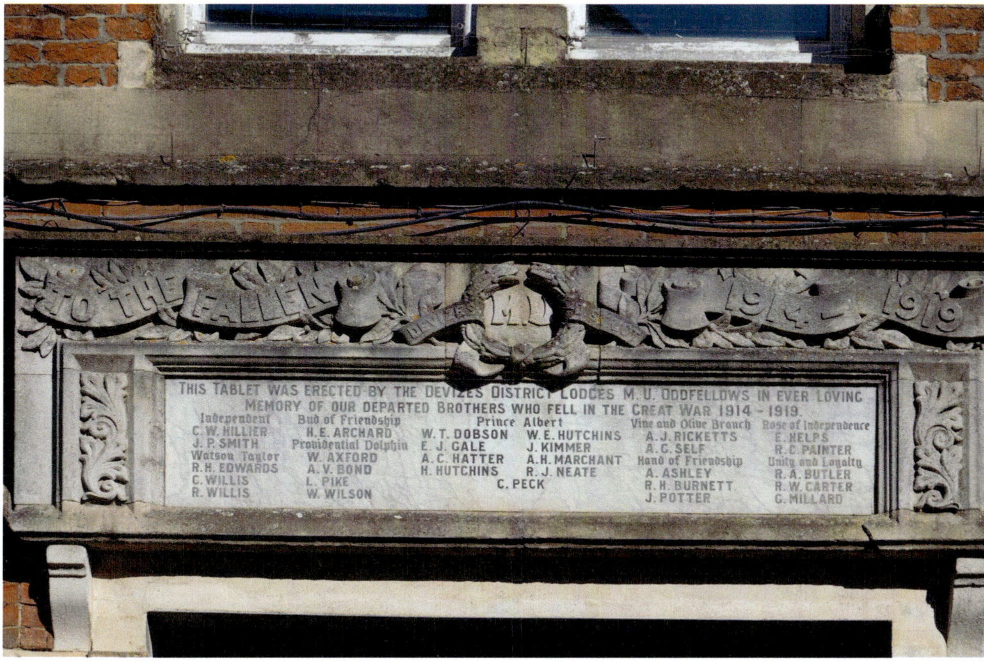

The sombre memorial to the fallen members of the League of Oddfellows.

Oddfellows Hall was constructed as a meeting place for the society in 1873, designed in a clearly visible Gothic Revival style. Prior to the building of the hall, the local Oddfellows lodge had met at the local Rising Sun public house. From 1882 until the early years of the twentieth century, the building was also used as a working men's club and until recently the ground floor housed a branch of Halifax bank.

The building was given listed status in 1972.

Old Town Hall

Standing on the corner of Wine Street is a grand Georgian building of Bath stone known today as the Old Town Hall. The front face is dominated by a large clock flanked by two carved-stone cherubs among a floral-style decoration below a bold carving of the Devizes coat of arms. This ornate top piece sits above four tall windows on each face of the building, separated by details of semi-recessed columns. Below them, the building is finished in a rusticated style with four arched openings on an arcade of similar positioning to first-floor windows. The side facing St John's Street effectively repeats the front, which faces Market Street, but in a far simpler style. The columns are rendered in a square, almost sketched, style.

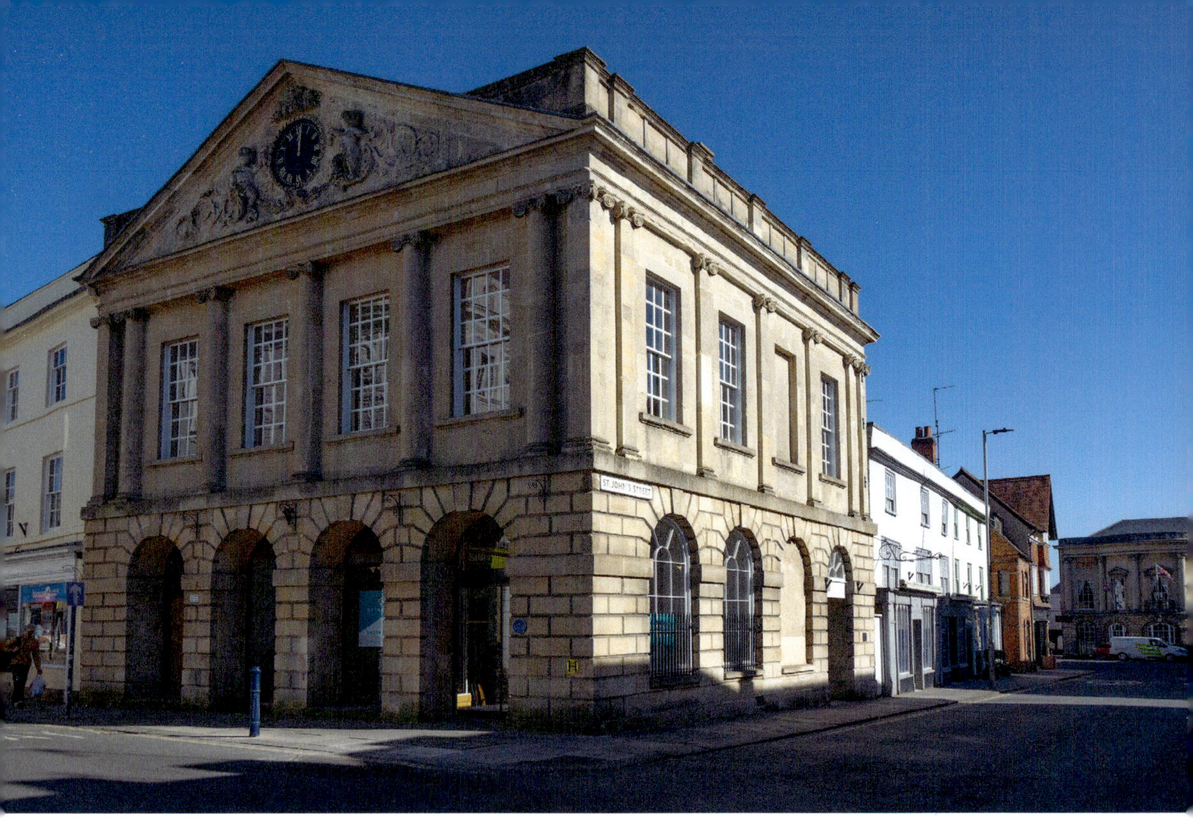

The Old Town Hall on St John's Street.

Designed by an architect named Lawrence and built between 1750 and 1752, it was completed in 1753, as is shown on the blue plaque the building proudly wears. The building itself has had a long and varied life with many occupants. It was originally designed to be a cheese and poultry market for the town (the cheese vaults still remain intact below the current building) and market hall. Between 1785 and 1787, the upper room would become a depot and weapons store for the local militia. Later, it would see service as mess room for the officers of the Devizes Loyal Volunteers before occasionally being used as a Sunday school.

It was used as the Town Hall between 1806 and 1808 while the current one was being constructed. When it was finished in 1808, the council moved into their new dedicated premises. Thereafter, this building would always forthwith be known as the 'Old Town Hall'. From 1848, it was used as a reading room and library by the Devizes Literary and Scientific Society.

The council sold the building in 1826. In 1836, Cunnington wine merchants used the cool vaults to store their wines and spirits, remaining there until well into the twentieth century.

Company founder Alfred Cunnington owned what is considered the first commercial telephone in the UK. Working from designs shown in an 1876 edition of *Scientific American* magazine reporting the invention of the telephone by Alexander Graham Bell, by 1877 he had created his own telephone exchange, linking first the upper and

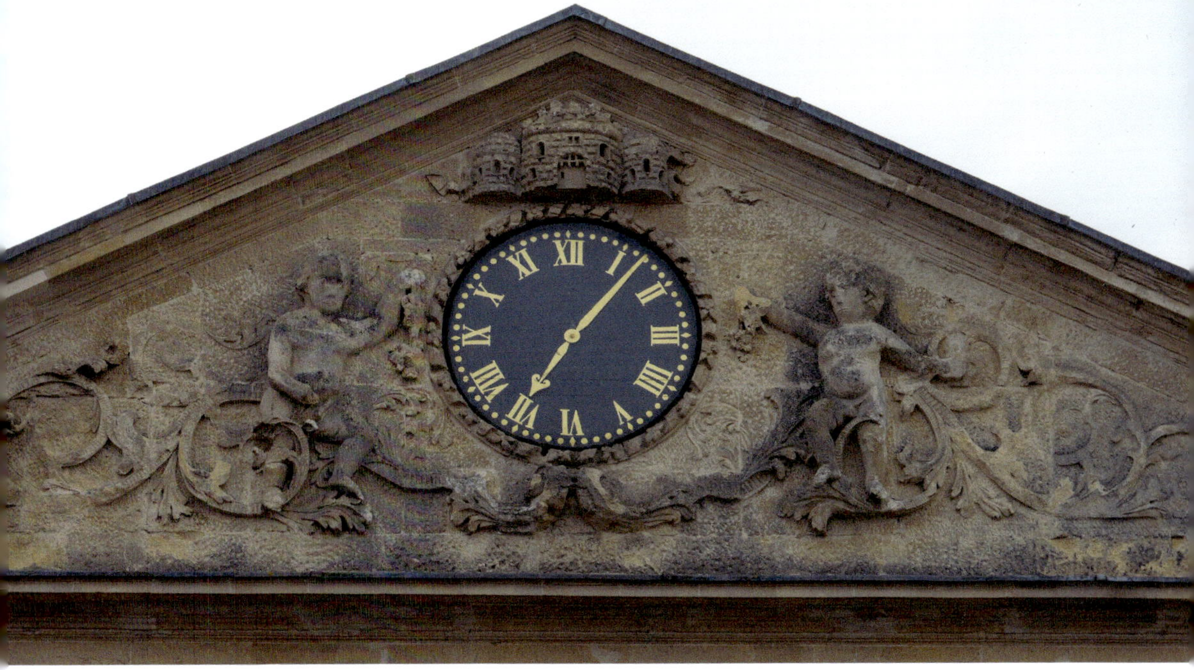

A detail of the clock and carvings atop the Old Town Hall.

lower floors of his wine merchant business with his home at Southgate House in another part of Devizes.

Despite complaints from locals, who claimed they could hear the voice of people using the phones when standing close to the wires, many people travelled to witness the unique invention from all over the country. The system was shown at a scientific exhibition at Devizes Town Hall in 1879 and again in 1900 at Edison's exhibition of electrical appliances in London. It was only dismantled when the National Telephone Company threatened Cunnington with legal action as his machine infringed their patents.

Much later, the building became a branch of the Cheltenham and Gloucester Building Society. It became a branch of the TSB bank in 2013 and finally closed as a financial institution in 2021. Until recently the building was occupied by the Hen House shop and art gallery, with one of the front archways being taken up a large iron cockerel in their honour. This prominent local business closed their doors late in 2024 and the ground floor is currently home to an auction house.

The whole building was listed in 1954. It was recorded as the 'Clock House Laundry' in the English Heritage listing for a number of years. The reason behind this is not known, but the story, if ever discovered, is likely to be fascinating.

P

Palace Cinema

The glorious art deco frontage of the Palace (or 'Picturedrome' as it is sometimes called) dominates one side of Northgate Street as you approach Market Place. The white front with black decorations and window frames is dominated by a pair of chaste female figures holding aloft illuminated glass torches. With one on each side of the front of the building standing on sturdy black brackets, they are a welcome change from the more exotic and less thoroughly dressed ladies frequently found on the architecture of 1930s cinemas. Their illuminated torches are repeated on a smaller scale within the building, attached to brass mountings. The cinema name stands bold above the covered entrance in sans-serif letters, with bulbs on the centre line of each letter spelling them out after dark.

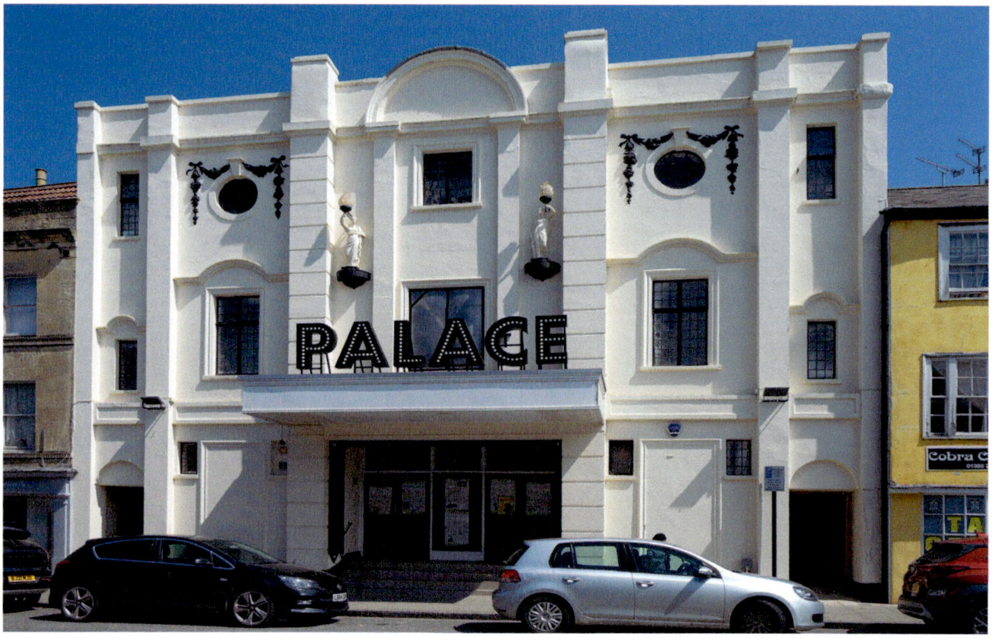

The Palace cinema on Northgate Street.

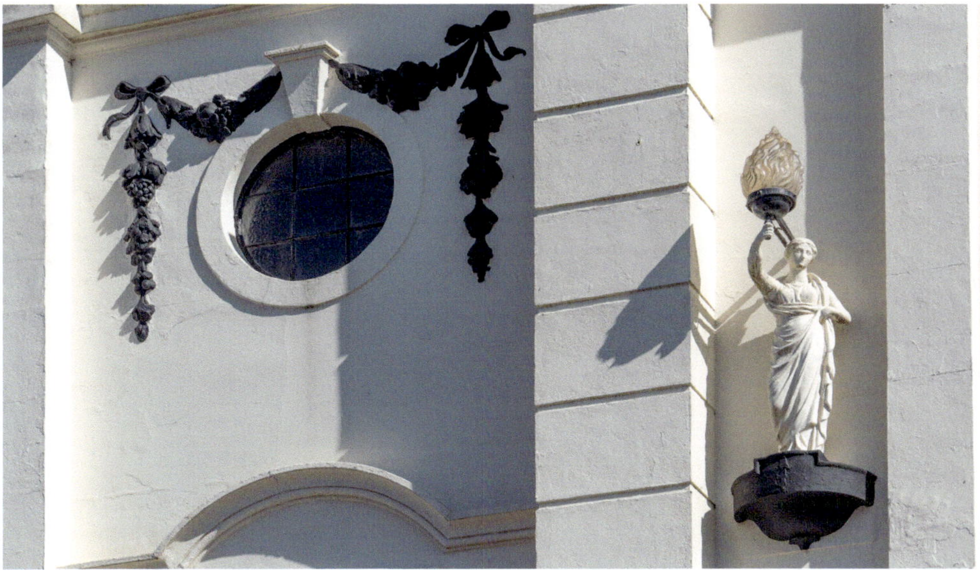

The chaste figure and grand front window of the Palace cinema.

The first cinema on this site was built in 1912 under the name the Picture Palace. This was later enlarged in the 1920s to become the Electric Palace, the capacity growing from 417 to 900 seats. It was further extended and modified into the current form in 1932 to a design by Ernest Roberts of Satchwell and Roberts from Birmingham. During this time, it was independently operated by A. Austin Pilkington Theatres, who also owned the now sadly demolished Regal Cinema which once stood once opposite the Castle Hotel in Devizes.

In 1975, the cinema was acquired by Zetters and split into a smaller auditorium in the former circle for films and a bingo club beneath. It was later operated by Miles Byrne until his death in 1986, then taken over by Steven Wischusen until 1992 when it became part of the Robins Cinemas chain. Still later, it was operated by Angel Bingo under the banner name of Angel Leisure, which was under the ownership of John Angel.

The cinema was closed for renovation in 2021 and Angel Bingo was closed in 2022 with a view to it being reinstated as a second cinema screen or as a live performance venue. Press reports spoke of an investment of 'over a million pounds to reverse fifty years of decay' under the ownership of Picturedrome Cinemas with an avowed aim to keep it viable for 'the next one hundred years'.

Parnella House

Built around 1740, Parnella House stands on Market Place and might be missed as you walk past were it not for the oversized statue of Aesculapius that stands prominently

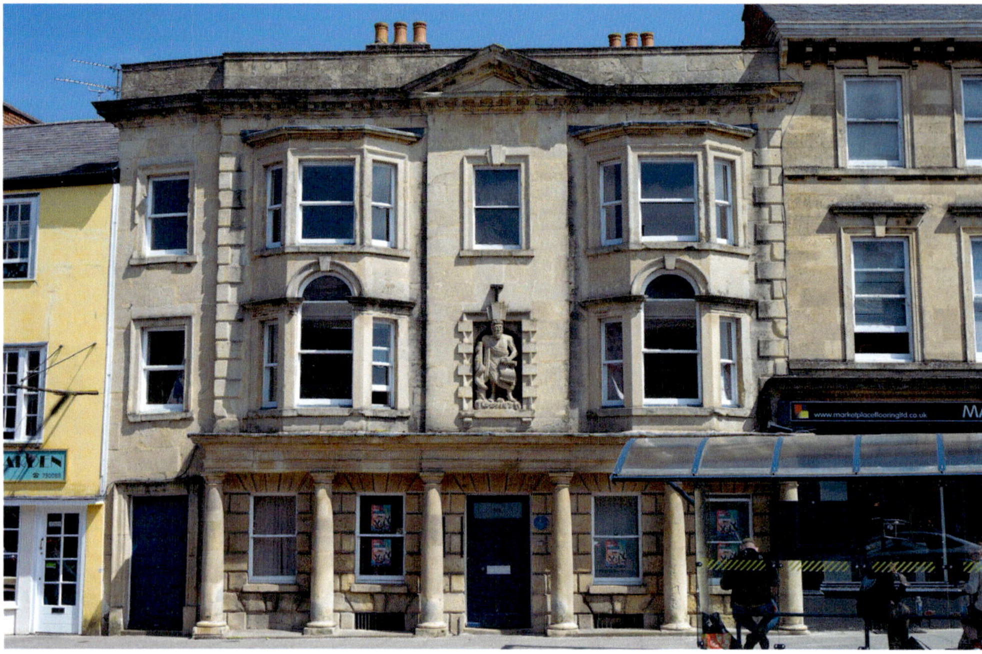

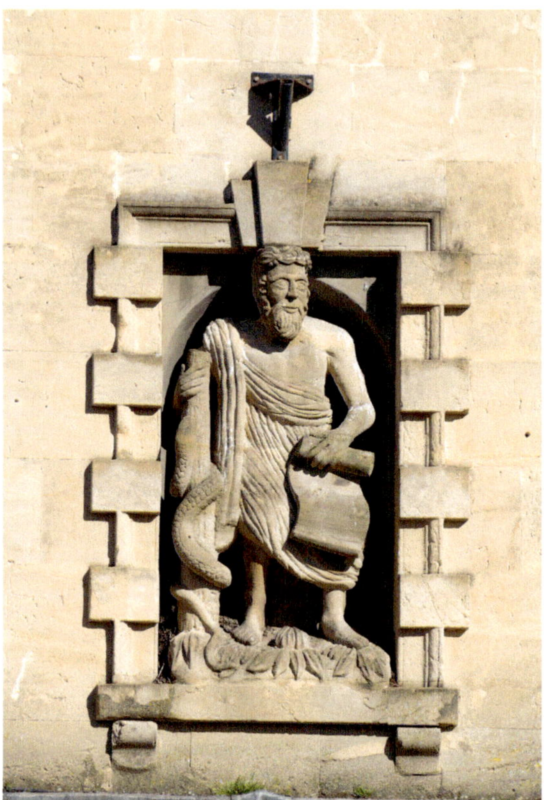

Above: Parnella House, Market Place.

Left: The grand figure of the Greek god Aesculapius on Parnella House.

within a niche above the bold blue doorway surrounded by an ornate Bath stone building front.

The Greek god Aesculapius, son of Apollo, was a hero and the god of medicine whose powers extended to healing and the raising of the dead. He is depicted here holding the staff of Aesculapius, a wooden staff with a serpent coiled around it, a traditional symbol of medicine. Unusually, on this statue there is only one snake, while classically the staff typically has two intertwined serpents. The staff features within the badge of the British army's Royal Army Medical Corps and numerous other medical insignias. This statue is also holding an unfurled scroll that is said to represent knowledge.

The statue of Aesculapius was adding during the early nineteenth century, when the building was occupied by a surgeon named W. Claire. He replaced the centre upstairs window with the niche and statue.

The building itself contains a mixture of architectural styles. The ground floor is in a rusticated style fronted by six free-standing columns that support a classic temple-style addition built against the original wall. Upstairs are Venetian-style windows topped by a tiny triangular pediment.

There was significant local uproar when a prominent bus shelter was erected in front of the building in the early twenty-first century, but on this rare occasion passenger comfort was placed before an uninterrupted view of the building, and the bus shelter was constructed. It still stands today.

In common with many buildings in Devizes, it was given listed status in 1954.

Pyramid

The *Devizes Pyramid* stands on Sidmouth Street, on the courtyard of Albion Place. Created in 2008 and sculpted by Richard Cowdy of Calne, it was given to the town of Devizes in 2008 by Patrick and Joan Norton.

The pyramid is cast in bronze and stands on a concrete plinth that continues the lines of the bronze pyramid on top. Devizes stands at the meeting point of three major manor boundaries: Rowde, Potterne and Bishops Cannings. In recognition of this, the pyramid is cast with three sides, as distinct from the classic model with a square base.

Each face of the pyramid is decorated with cast engravings of scenes around or considered relevant to the town. One face is taken up by an image of the original Norman castle that led to the foundation of Devizes in around AD 1100; another by a rendition of a narrow boat climbing the Caen Hill Locks; and the final is of various breeds of sheep and a fine ram's head below a rendition of the castle keep, recalling the contribution that wool and fabric weaving made to the Devizes economy. Around the base is the legend 'The Wealth of Wiltshire Founded on Wool'.

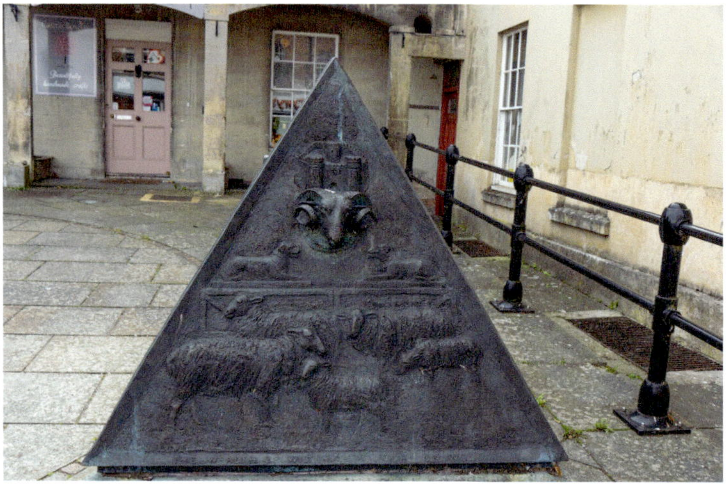

One face of the *Devizes Pyramid* on Sidmouth Street. This face commemorates the local wool industry.

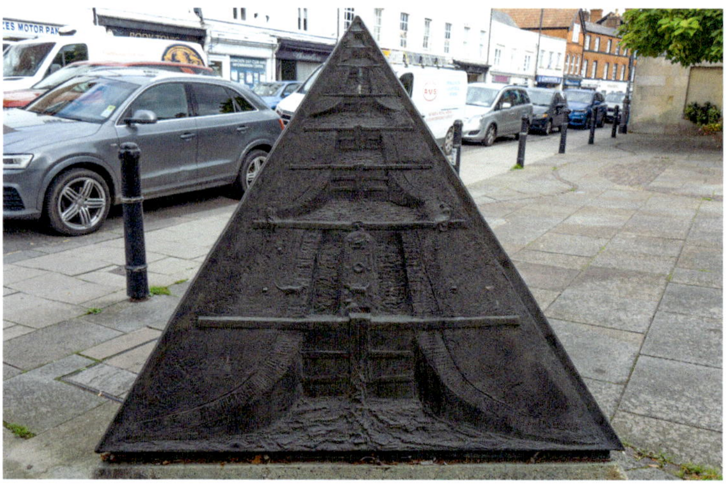

This face commemorates the Caen flight of locks.

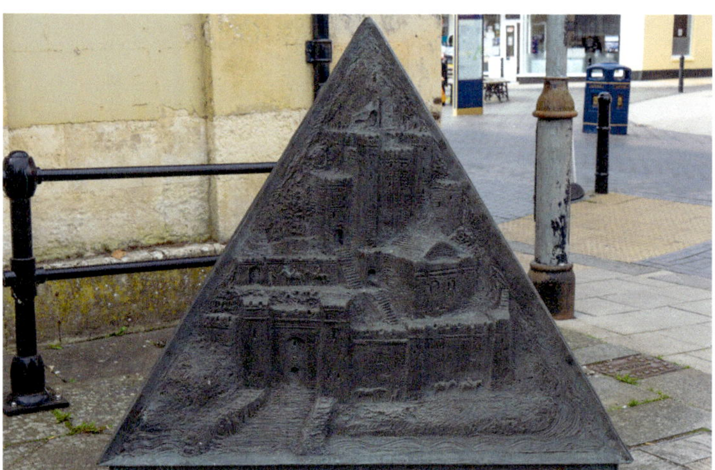

This one commemorates the Norman Castle at the heart of Devizes.

Q

Quaker Meeting House

As you walk along Devizes High Street you may notice a curiously plain-looking house made of traditional Bath stone among the retail properties. This sober-looking building dates back to 1702 and was originally built as a meeting house for the Religious Society of Friends, more commonly known as the Quakers.

The Quakers first arrived in Devizes during the 1650s when they still called themselves the Friends of Truth. William Penn, one of their early figureheads and one of their first Publishers of Truth, reported addressing a large meeting at the Market Hall in Devizes. He would go on to name and found the American colony of Pennsylvania when King Charles II granted him the lands in 1861 in lieu of debts owed to Penn's family.

Persecuted like many small religions under King Charles II, many Quakers chose to flee England and set up home in Pennsylvania under Penn, where freedom of religion was permitted and fellow Quakers were welcomed.

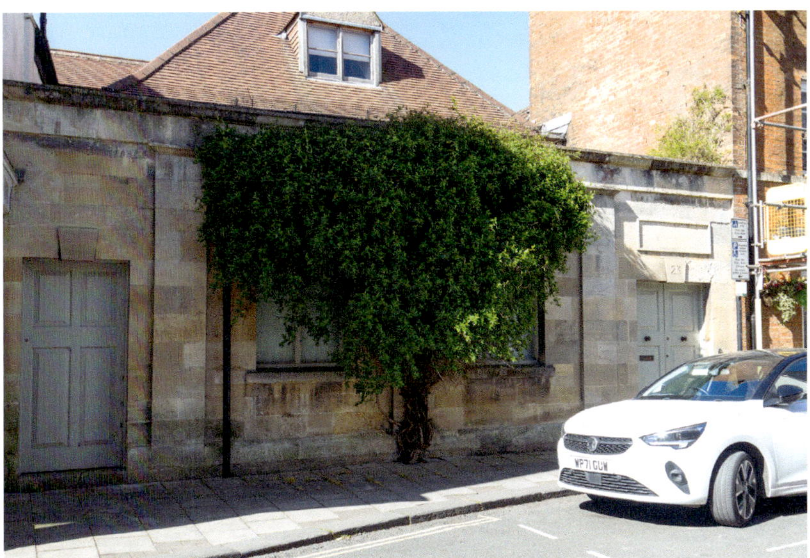

The private home that was once the Quaker Meeting house on High Street.

Following the passing of the Act of Toleration in 1689, the Quakers built a meeting house in the grounds of what is now Hillworth Park. The building itself is sadly long gone, but the Quaker burial ground that stood with it still remains.

Outgrowing this first meeting house, the Quakers built the building you see now on High Street in 1702. It remained in constant use until 1926 when numbers dwindled and the building was sold to become a private house.

Quaker worship began again in Devizes during the late 1970s. In 1994, a new, more modern meeting house was built, which remains in use to this day.

Quakers Walk

Quakers Walk is a smooth, tree-lined path that runs for approximately a mile from the Kennet and Avon Canal in Devizes to Roundway village along part of the historic Wessex Ridgeway Trail, which runs from Marlborough to Lyme Regis. A long-standing historic path, some believe it dates back to the reign of King Edward I.

The path was initially across what was known as New Park, a 130-acre deer park established in 1157. Very early maps describe the path as 'Keepers Walk', presumably referring to a path used by the new keeper of the deer park. No one is entirely sure how it came to be known as Quakers Walk, but the Quakers themselves believe it was because many of their members lived in the village of Bishops Cannings and used this path to come to their meetings in Devizes.

While there were no doubt earlier buildings, it was most famously the location of a grand James Wyatt-designed house for James and Eleanor Sutton from 1780. In common with so many great houses after the First World War, the house fell into disrepair. It was demolished by the county council immediately after the Second World War and the estate was broken up and sold off. Only the converted stables remain today.

Maps showing the footpath as a public right of way exist as far back as 1817, when the lord of the manor arranged for the footpath to be legally moved. His aim was to make it both further from his house and for the walk to be easier by allowing walkers to go around rather than over a steep hill. A print exists today from a glass negative dated 1890 showing the tree-lined path looking very similar to the way it does today. The walk starts at a magnificent set of gates and lodge (both given listed status in 1987), which once marked the entrance and edge of the estates of Lord Roundway. It is an easy path to follow, with the option to continue to the battle site at Roundway Down (see p. 67). Quakers Road runs off the end of Quakers Walk into a new estate where, among other things, you will find the new Wiltshire Police headquarters.

Architectural historians believe that the urns currently on top of the gateposts are not the originals; instead, they are believed to have come from Whitton Park in Twickenham, Middlesex, home of the first Lady Roundway.

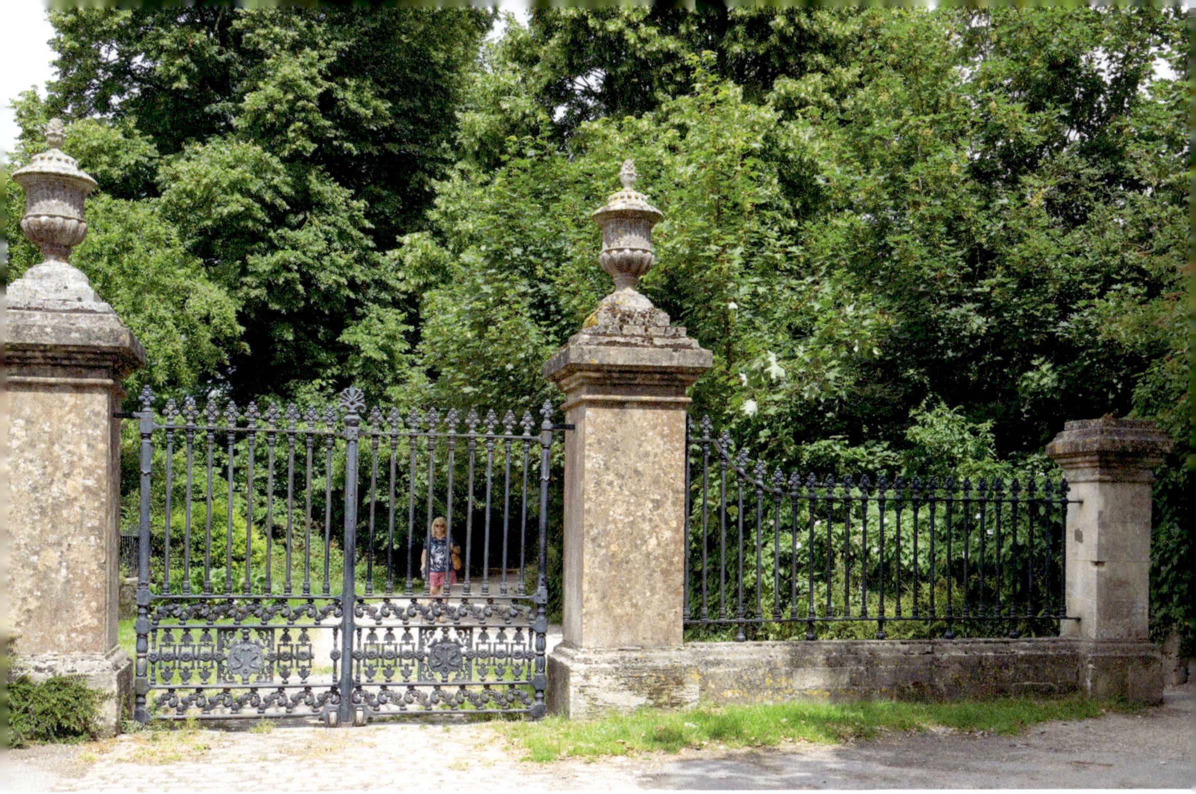

Above: The grand gated entrance to Quakers Walk.

Right: The urns atop the entrance to Quakers Walk are believed to have come from Whitton Park.

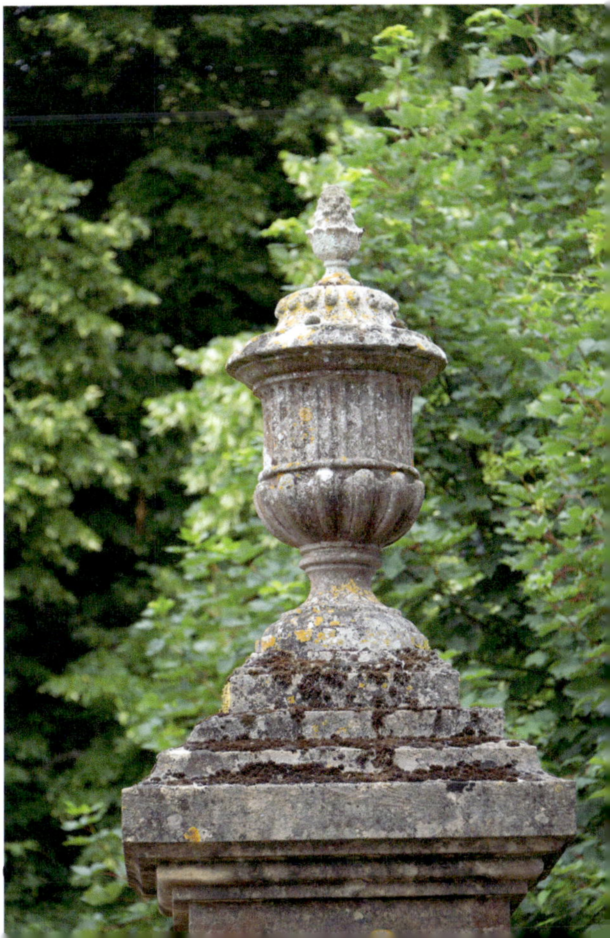

R

Ruth Pierce

The remarkable local incident of Ruth Pierce was recorded by coroner John Clare on 26 January 1753. According to the document, a 'great quarrel' arose between four women: Elizabeth Slade, Sarah Slade, Mary Parker and Ruth Pierce. Together they had purchased a sack of grain from farmer Nathanial Alexander at the corn market for 17*s*.

When money was collected to pay for the grain, Ruth Pierce was accused of not having handed over her share. In the face of this accusation, she is reported to have

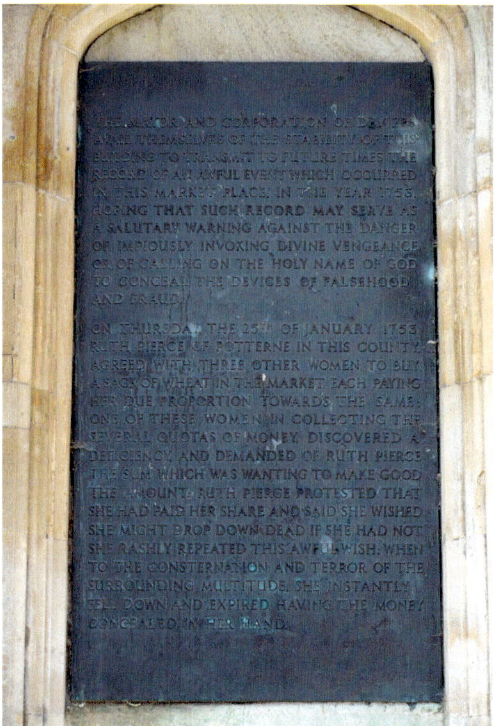

The great bronze plaque on the Market Cross telling the tale of Ruth Pierce.

called upon the Almighty as her witness and wished that she might drop down dead that minute if she had not paid her due. This rash wish was repeated a second time and immediately 'from the Visitation of the Great and Almighty God' she was struck down. As no marks of injury or violence appeared on her body, the jurors reporting on the matter assigned the cause to be 'accidental death'. Upon her demise, her missing share of the money was found concealed in her hand.

This remarkable event is recorded for all to see on a large plaque mounted on the side of Market Cross. It is a cautionary tale not to rashly call upon God as your witness.

Public interest in this legally recorded event continued for many years, and postcards of her home in Potterne continued to be available well into the twentieth century with details of the tale upon them.

Roundway Down

Roundway Down is a steep-sided hill approximately 2 miles to the north-east of Devizes that is the home of an Iron Age hill fort. It was the site of the Battle of Roundway Down on 13 July 1643, considered by some the most important Royalist victory of the English Civil War.

After the hard-fought Battle of Lansdown, near Bath, Royalist General Hopton retreated to Devizes hoping to receive reinforcements from their garrison at Oxford. The pursuing Parliamentarian General Sir Willima Waller deployed on Roundway Down and laid siege to Devizes with a Parliamentarian army of 5,000 men.

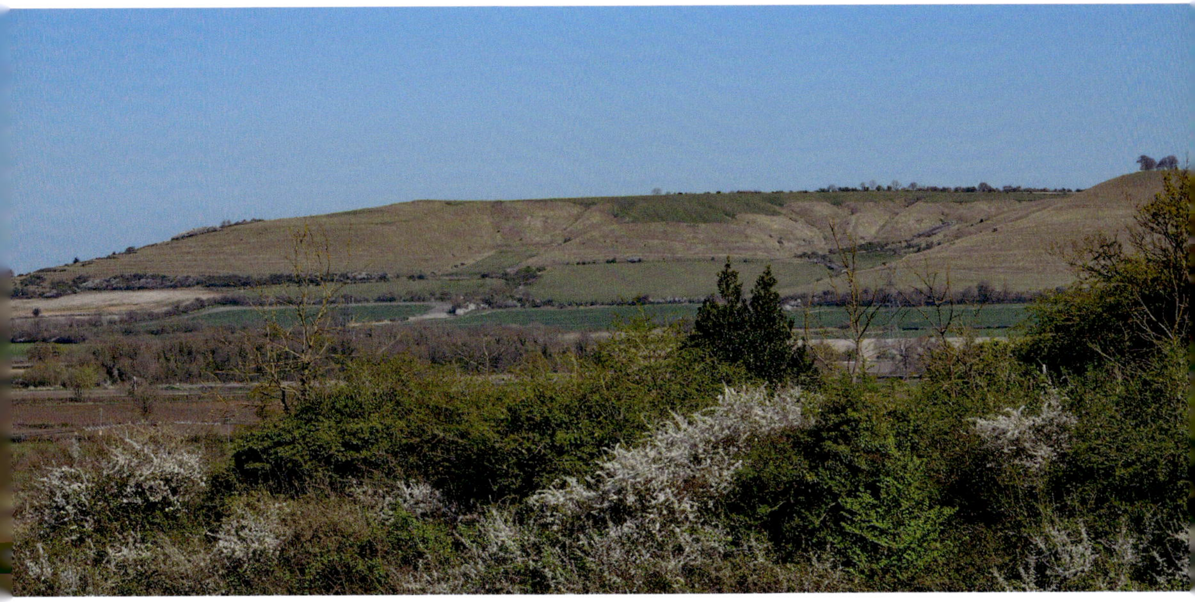

Roundway Down, where an English Civil War battle was fought.

Desperate for the reinforcements and supplies, 300 cavalrymen under Prince Maurice were despatched to Oxford, leaving 3,000 men to hold Devizes. Prince Maurice found a large part of the Royalist army, including the king, absent from Oxford, but accepting the call for aid, Lord Wilmot marched immediately with two brigades of the experienced 'Oxford cavalry' and a third joined him at Marlborough. In total, over 1,500 cavalry set out to aid the forces at Devizes.

Despite having ridden all night, Lord Wilmot launched an immediate attack on Roundway Down, seeing the Parliamentarian deployment incomplete with units out of line. The Parliamentarian cavalry stood to meet the charge, hoping to drive it off with fire from their carbines. They were swept from the field, being hotly pursued by Lord Wilmot. So thorough was their rout that many rode over a 300-foot-deep precipice into an area now known as 'the bloody ditch'.

Seeing the battle taking place nearby, the Royalist garrison in Devizes moved towards Roundway Down and the Parliamentarians found themselves with this force advancing towards their rear. Forming a square, they withdrew to the north-west in good order until the Royalist cavalry returned from their pursuit, captured the Parliamentarian artillery and turned it on their retreating force. The retreat turned into a rout and the Royalist army was victorious.

The victory at Roundway Down enabled the Royalist cause to capture the port of Bristol two weeks later, which allowed them to bring supplies into the area and make contact with their allies in Ireland. The Royalists would retain control of the south-west of England for the next two years, only losing control of the area in late 1645.

The old Iron Age hill fort on top of Roundway Down is now referred to as 'Oliver's Castle' after Oliver Cromwell, the leader of the Parliamentarian New Model Army, but he was not present at the battle and likely never visited the site.

S

Sergeant Rogers Way

In one of the new estates on the east side of Devizes, you will find yourself looking at a map of streets with names inspired by military sources. There is a Waller Road, named after Parliamentarian General William Waller, and Hopton Road, named after Ralph Hopton, a Royalist general. Opening off the latter is Sergeant Rogers Way, named after a humble and more recent military figure.

Sergeant Maurice Albert Windham Rogers, VC (Victoria Cross), MM (Military Medal) of the Second Battalion of the Wiltshire Regiment is a local hero who fell in the Battle of Anzio on 3 June 1944.

He was awarded his VC posthumously after making a lone advance against a strongly held enemy position behind barbed wire at Ardea. According to an account in the *London Gazette*, he advanced while firing his Thompson submachine gun and throwing grenades until he was 100 yards ahead of his platoon and 30 yards beyond

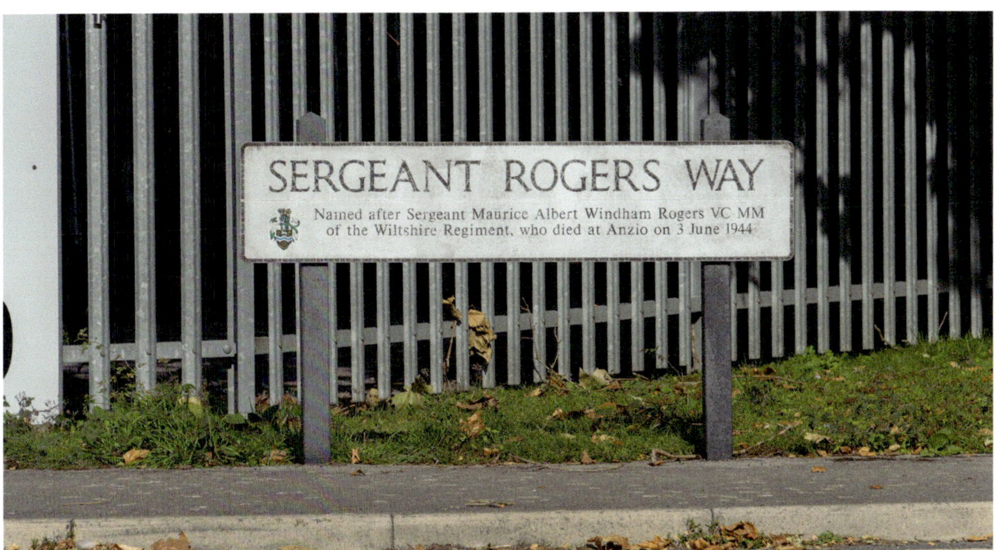

Sergeant Rogers Way commemorates a modern local military hero.

the enemy's defensive barbed wire. Under fire from seven machine guns, he destroyed two before being shot down at point blank range.

His actions both drew the enemy's fire and inspired the other members of his platoon to advance and take the position. His actions were, to quote the *London Gazette*, 'In the highest tradition of the British army'.

Shambles Market

The main Bath stone entrance to the Shambles Market stands on the eastern corner of Market Place. The high and airy market hall is entered through a tall, arched doorway flanked by a pair of arched windows. Directly above the doorway stands a square clock tower mounting an ornate clock, marked out with Roman numerals and ornate gold hands. Atop this, at the pinnacle of the building, is an ornate weathervane.

Inside it is easy to imagine the location of the original market stalls' layout, which would have run the length of the building to left and right of the centre walkway. The upper galleries are supported on each side by a line of metal stanchions set atop a smooth flagstone floor, and above those is a clearly visible wooden roof.

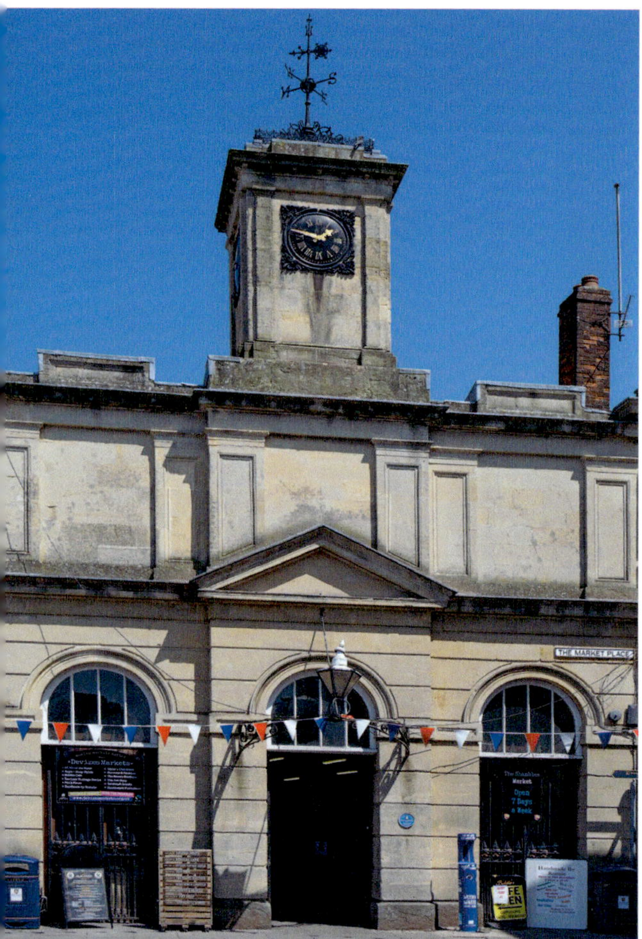

The grand front and clock tower of the Shambles Market.

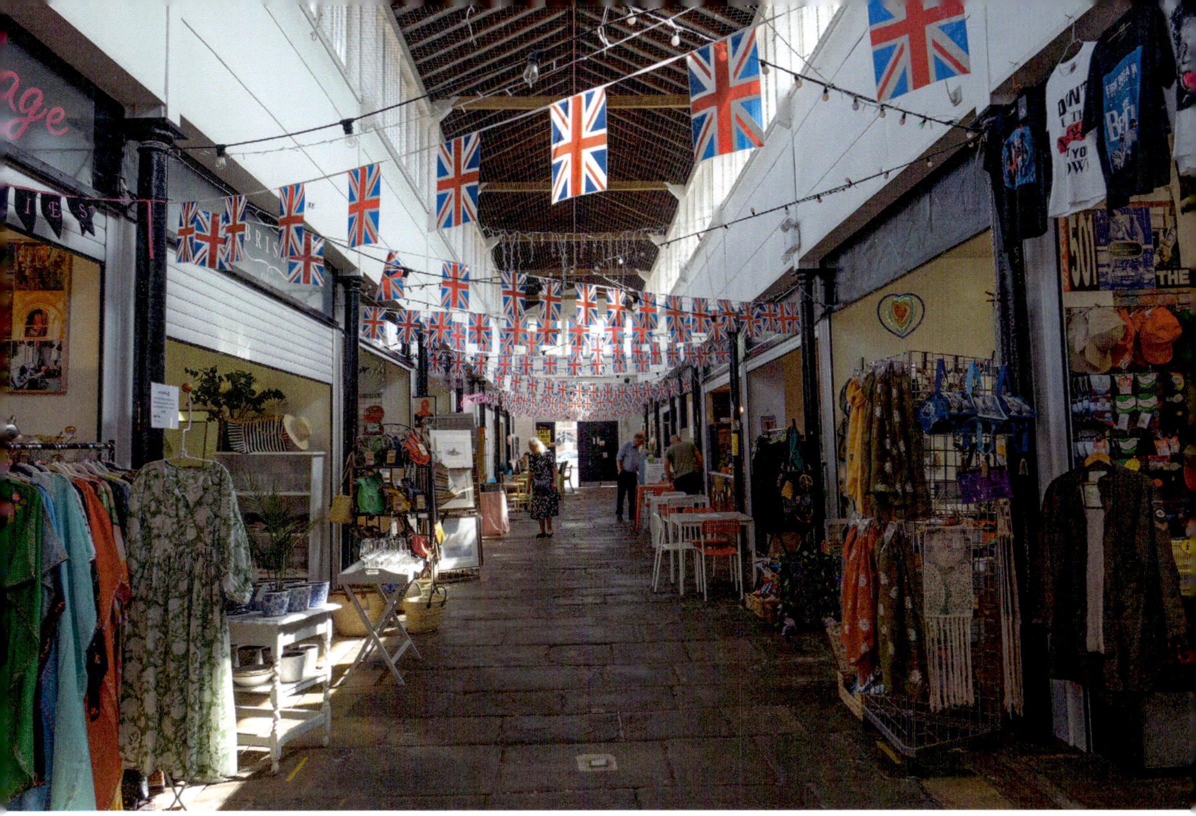

The stalls and period flagstone floor of the Shambles Market.

The rear of the building is a simple red-brick affair, opening onto a car park. The three arches of the front are repeated on a much smaller scale, with a central door and two faux arches to the left and right and a Victorian-style iron lantern above the door.

The front and rear of the interior are on different levels, with front being known as the Lower Hall and the rear as the Upper Hall. Currently, permanent shops and businesses occupy the Upper Hall with the space in the Lower Hall used more for the stalls on market day and other events.

Initially the site of a medieval butchers' market, the current building was constructed in 1835 as a butchery and provisions market, and is marked on the first-generation Ordnance Survey maps as 'Market House'.

On the archway above the walkway, between the Upper and Lower Halls, is a full-colour 3D rendition of the Devizes coat of arms sculpted into the stonework, below which is 'A. D. 1838', the year the building was completed.

On a wall above the heads of the stalls, dated 6 November 1862, is a board proclaiming the 'Rules of the Cheese Market' for traders detailing timings, the ringing of the market bell and, showing some things never change, rules about the parking of carts during market hours.

The building's use has changed over the years, today becoming used for more general retail purposes. Inside, you will find antique stalls, crafts, locally produced food and a fine and busy café to the rear of the building. On the traditional Thursday

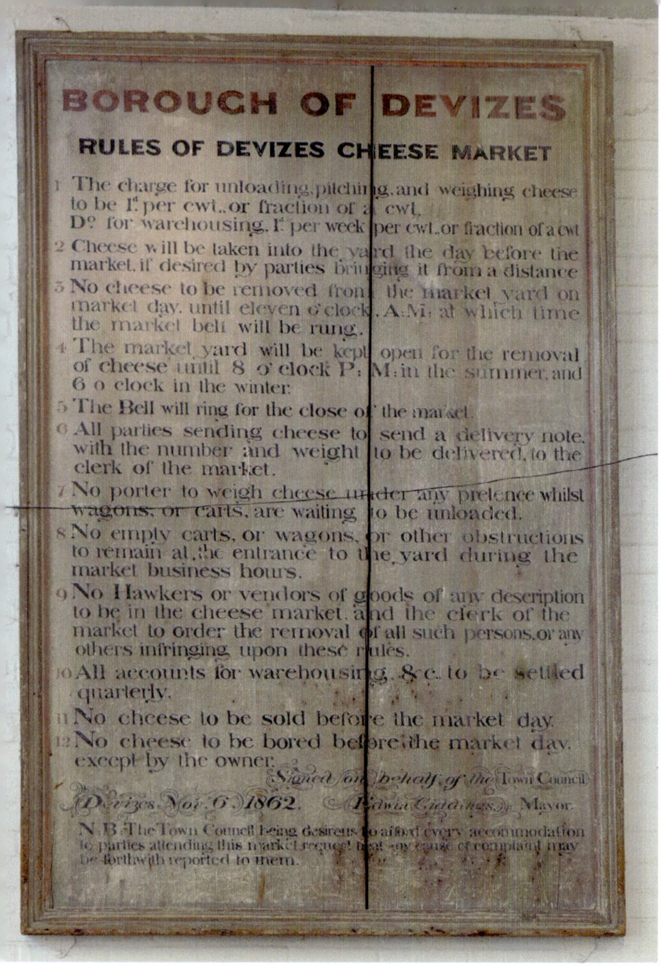

The rules of the Devizes cheese market from 1862.

market, the open spaces within the Lower Hall fill up with traders offering a wide range of goods.

The building was awarded listed status in 1972.

St James' Church

Standing on Church Walk and backing onto the Crammer, St James' Church, more than any other, stands physically in the centre of Devizes life.

The church started life as a chapel of ease for Bishops Cannings and was likely built on the site of an older chapel, but this had disappeared by 1338. The current church's exact date of construction is unknown, but it is first mentioned in records in 1461.

Initially referred to as being located on the green, St James' Church was often referred to as 'the Green Church' in early documents. Of those early days, sadly only the central tower remains. This tower is, however, regarded as a fine upright structure and houses a medieval tierceron vault.

It's formal dedication to St James occurred in 1505. Aside from the tower, the current church was built in 1831–32 to a design by John Peniston of Salisbury and

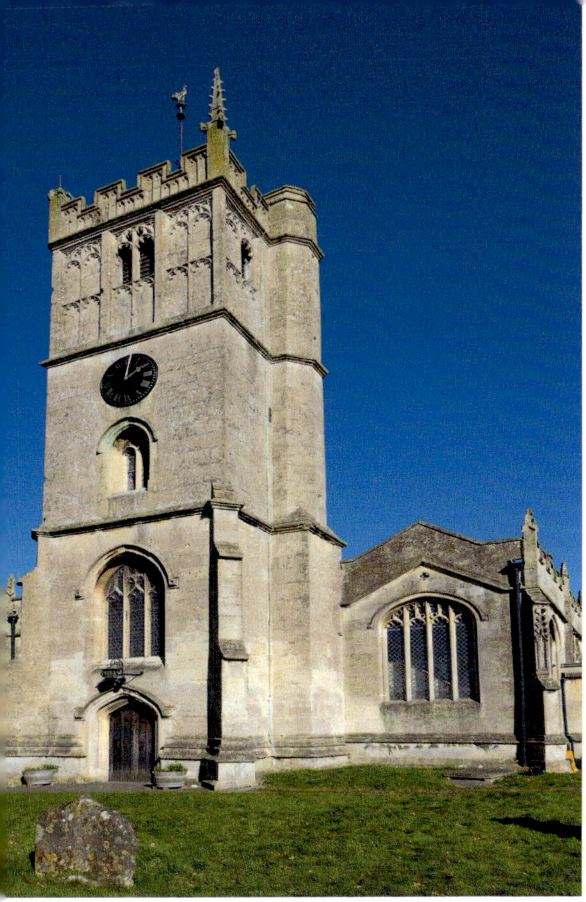

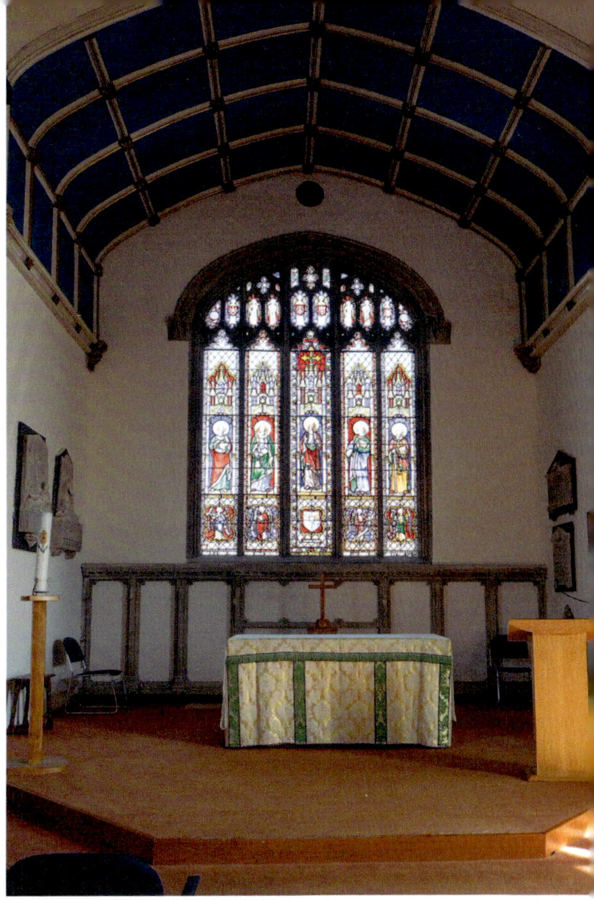

Above left: The tower of St James' Church.

Above right: The grand windows and thoroughly modern interior of St James' Church.

Benoni White in a Gothic Revival style using parts of the old medieval stonework as bases for new walls. The interior was remodelled by Peter Kent in 2008 to include such unexpected refinements as a carpet.

When the Le Marchant Barracks was completed and occupied in 1878, St James' became the official garrison church of the Wiltshire Regiment, and technically remains so to this day; in fact, some of their colours (flags) can be found on display there.

At the end of the church's south aisle are two finely polished brass plaque war memorials to the fallen of the Wiltshire Regiment in the Anglo-Zulu War of 1879 and to men lost fighting in India between 1882 and 1886.

When there were fears subsidence would cause the churchyard of St James' to slide into the waters of the Crammer, for general public safety a 4-foot-high restraining wall was erected in 1969 between the churchyard and the Crammer despite huge public opposition. However, the churchyard and the waters of the Crammer remain apart to this day, so it may be judged a success on the basis of results.

The church was listed in 1954.

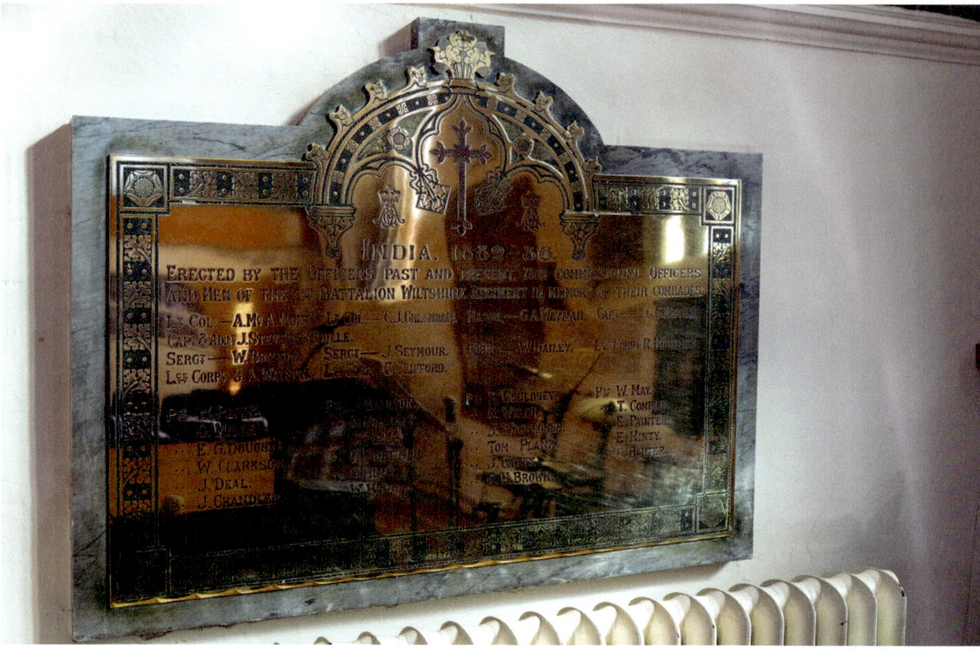

A treasured and well-polished memorial to those of the Wiltshire Regiment who fell during action in India in 1882–86.

St John the Baptist Church

St John's Church is set off Long Street and stands alongside the splendid Devizes war memorial, which the church lost part of its churchyard to accommodate.

St John's Church was built in the twelfth century under the auspices of the Bishops of Salisbury as the official church of the garrison and governor of Devizes Castle. While greatly expanded over the years, a considerable amount of the original building remains and is considered some of the finest Norman architecture still extant in the UK.

Hubert de Burgh fled to the church from Devizes Castle to claim sanctuary in 1233 and was illegally dragged back to the castle. After an appeal to the bishop, he was restored to sanctuary and a stockade was built around the church to keep him safe. He was rescued by his followers from the church soon after.

Facing towards the church from Long Street, to the left side of the building is the large and very ornate Beauchamp Chapel, resembling the Beauchamp and Tocotes Chapel at Bromham. To the north end of the building is the smaller North Chapel.

The church is constructed from ashlar Bath stone and has two chapels, a large and unusual oblong-shaped crossing tower with a taller stair turret at one corner standing 65 feet high, and magnificent north and south porches.

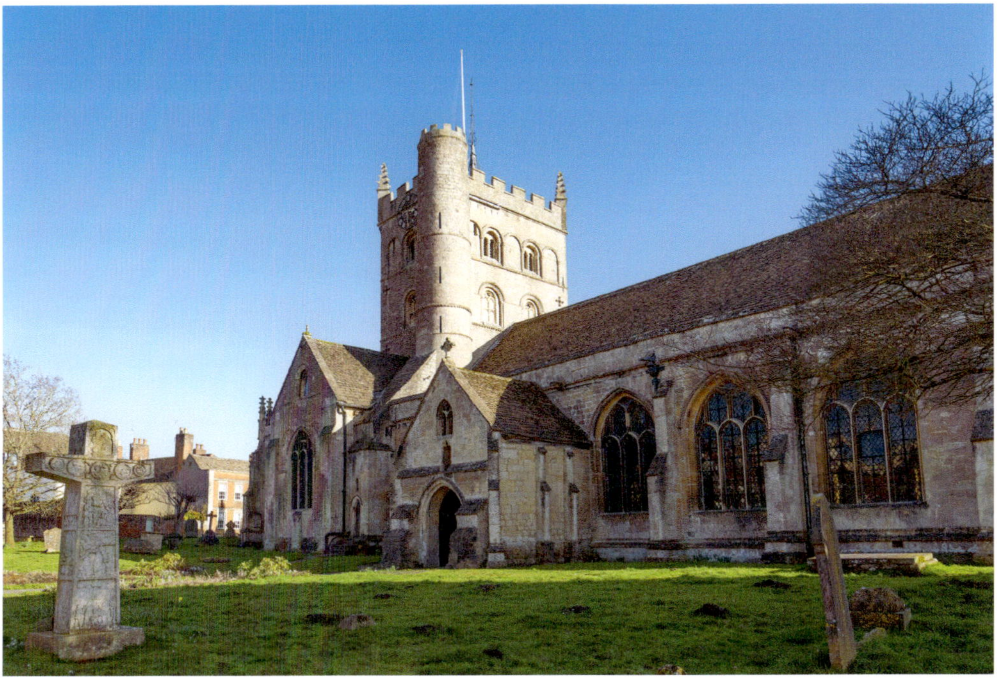

St John the Baptist Church with the Millennium Cross in the foreground.

The tower is richly decorated both inside and out. Once a plain-roofed design, when the church was largely rebuilt in the fifteenth century it gained the ornamental battlements it still wears today. The west side of the tower was rebuilt at some stage, likely as a result of damage during the English Civil War, and much of the interior decoration on that wall was not reinstalled. It would see more restoration work in 1922.

The front of the church still wears the marks of its involvement in the English Civil War: the impact of shot from a canister round on the east wall near the Beauchamp Window. A canister round, also known as grape shot, was a round fired from a small cannon made up of a container or canister containing around twenty musket balls (or grapes) designed to burst on exiting the muzzle of the cannon and spread widely, in a similar style to the shot of a smoothbore shotgun for use against infantry. Why this was fired against a building is unknown, but the marks remain.

The tower itself was used as a powder magazine during the English Civil War and lead from the roofs of both St John's and St Mary's was removed and melted down to make musket balls.

There are clear signs that the church that stands today is much enlarged from the twelfth-century original. There are weathered courses within stonework within that clearly imply there were chapels that once stood within the boundaries of the church footprint that stands today.

The church was the subject of a major rebuild in 1862–63 when the need for more space for parishioners became an issue. Directed by W. Slater of London under the

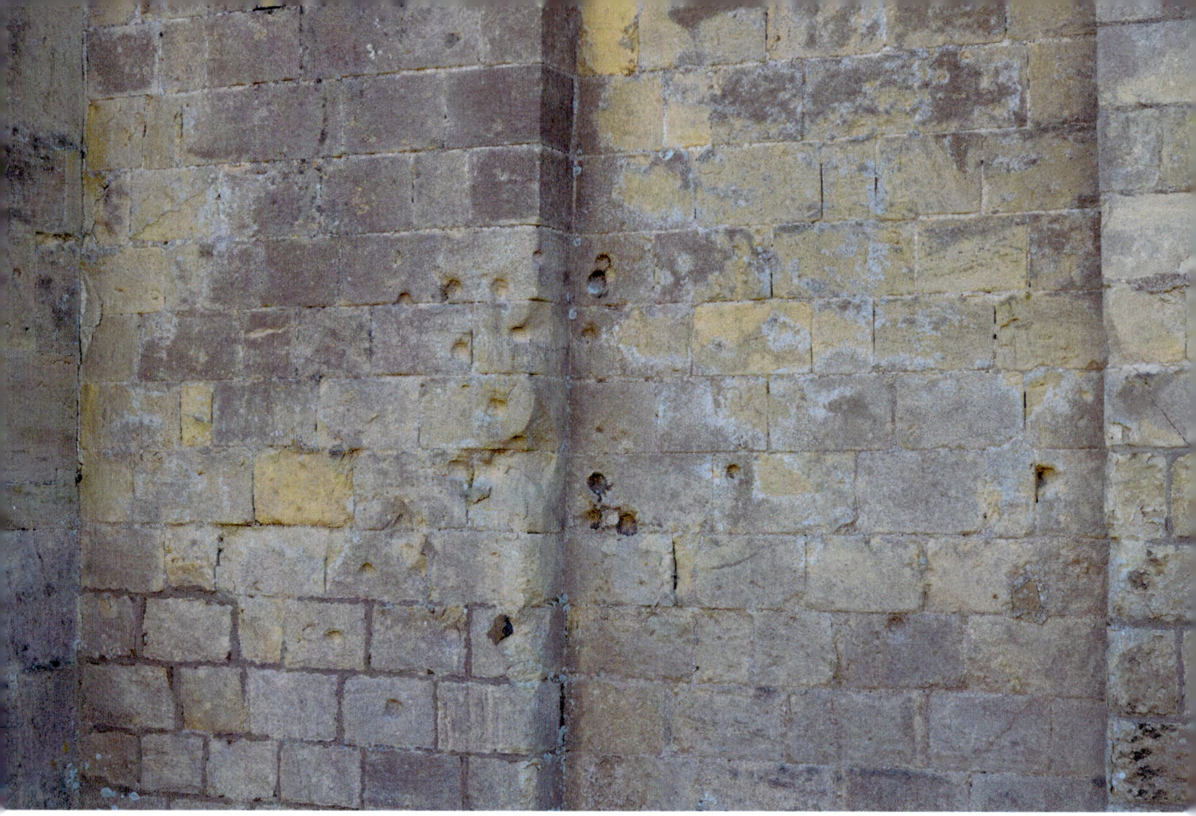

The results of a round of grapeshot being fired at St John the Baptist Church.

advice of Sir Gilbert Scott, the nave was extended by one bay to create 154 extra seating spaces. And the bowing west wall was rebuilt in the style of the fifteenth century to match much of the then current interior. The west gallery, already in a precarious state, was demolished.

During the Victorian era many large stained-glass windows were added as various windows were enlarged or even created during the various rebuilds and enlargements, the last being made as late as 1920.

'Corporation pews' were installed in the church around 1730 for the exclusive use of local dignitaries. As in many churches, they remained in place until 1971 when their concept was discontinued.

During 1902, more repair work was carried out on the church to bring the South Chapel back into service. The church organ, built by John Snetzler and installed in 1743, was moved back into the northern part of the church.

Following a fire in 2006 the organ was damaged beyond repair. The congregation was left with only an electric organ for accompaniment and an appeal was launched to repair or replace the damaged organ, supported by Mrs Sarah Rose Troughton DStJ, HM Lord Lieutenant of Wiltshire.

In 2023, a United Reformed Church in Plymouth closed and kindly donated their 1884 Hele and Son organ to St John's Church. Renowned organ builder Lance Foy and his team were tasked with rebuilding this instrument.

The original tower clock of St John's dated back to 1759. It was originally installed in the Old Town Hall and was presented to the church following the Town Hall's rebuilding. This would be replaced in 1901 by a new clock installed in honour of Queen Victoria.

In the churchyard, a cross was erected in 2000 to mark the arrival of the new millennium. Nearby is a sad memorial to five Potterne folk who drowned while rowing on Drews Pond on the Sabbath.

Like so many buildings in Devizes, the church was made a listed building in 1954.

St John's Alley

Running between High Street and St John's Street, St John's Alley is made up of a number of glorious jettied, wood-framed buildings commonly believed to have been built around 1550. Standing two or three storeys tall with their original brick and plaster filling still in place, they remain wonderfully well maintained.

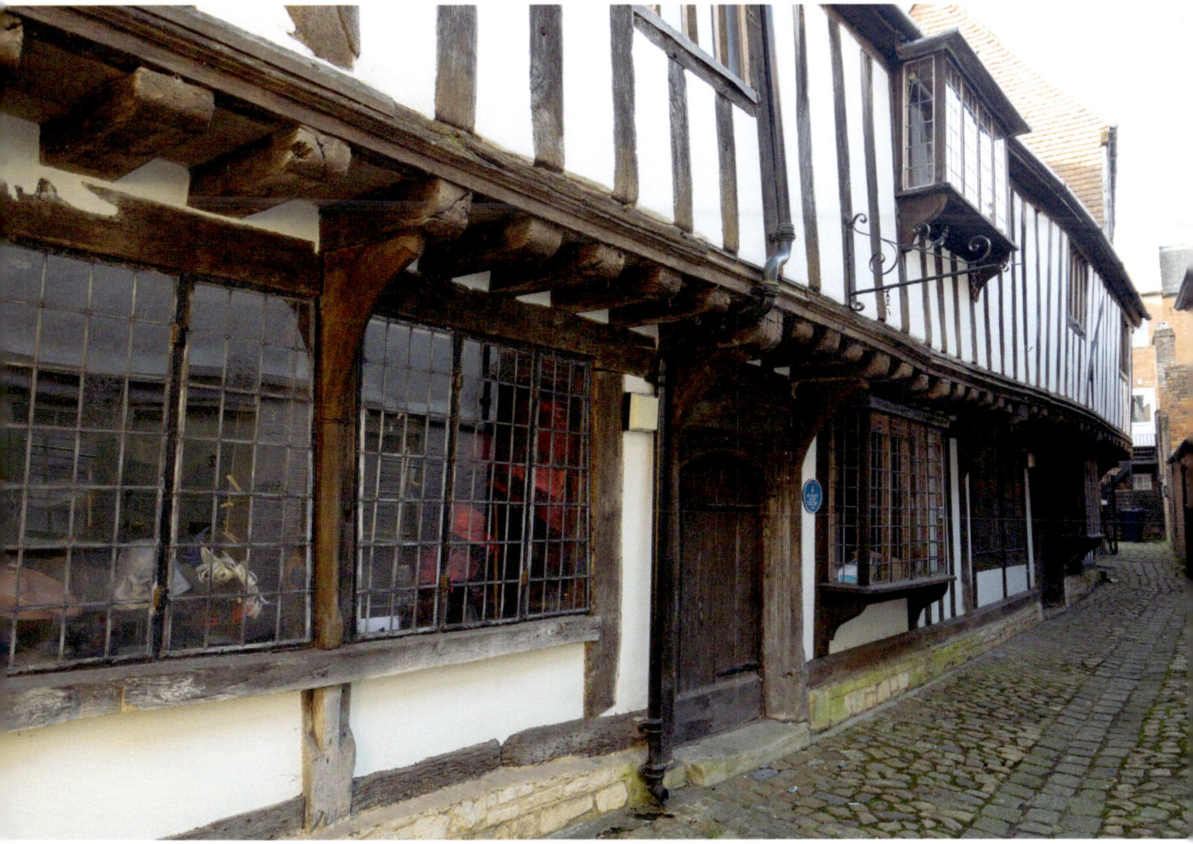

St John's Alley and its sixteenth-century, wood-framed buildings.

T

T. H. Southeron Estcourt Memorial Fountain

The Market Place in Devizes is awash with fascinating structures and listed buildings. One of the largest and most imposing structures is the T. H. Southeron Estcourt Memorial Fountain, which stands alongside the Market Cross in Market Place. It was designed and sculpted by Henry Woodyer and Carlo Nicoli.

The fountain was erected in 1879 as a memorial to T. H. Southeron Estcourt (1801 – 76) MP for Devizes between 1835 and 1844, raising to the lofty post of Home Secretary in 1859 under Henry John Temple, the Viscount Palmerston and founder of the Wiltshire Friendly Society in 1828. Friendly Societies were created to offer mutual support and financial aid to the poor of an area. Estcourt was first secretary to the society, later becoming president as he worked tirelessly towards the support of the poor of Devizes. His lifelong interest in this field led him to becoming the president of the Poor Law Board in 1858.

The fountain was funded by public subscription by the people of Devizes in memory of a man who was considered to have given the town so much. A small plaque to the rear of the fountain mentions a restoration anonymously funded in 1963 to the cost of £2,000. The fountain was restored again in 2007 with funds from the National Lottery and local man Mike Pitcher, a former pupil of Devizes Grammar school. Their respective efforts are commemorated on a bronze plaque set on top of what used to be one of the horse troughs around the old drinking fountain.

The fountain itself stands tall with a statue of the man himself atop a plinth decorated by floral carving. This is supported by four grouped cylindrical columns with ornate ironwork to support waterspouts running a stream of water into the upper basin, itself decorated by knotwork carvings. This upper structure is supported on several columns and the whole upper structure is standing on an octagonal stone base.

When full, bronze spouts surrounding the upper basin allow the surplus water to flow in a smooth stream to the lower basin, where there were once water troughs. All that remains of this now are blanked-off lion's head spouts that look out over seats and a commemorative bronze plaque.

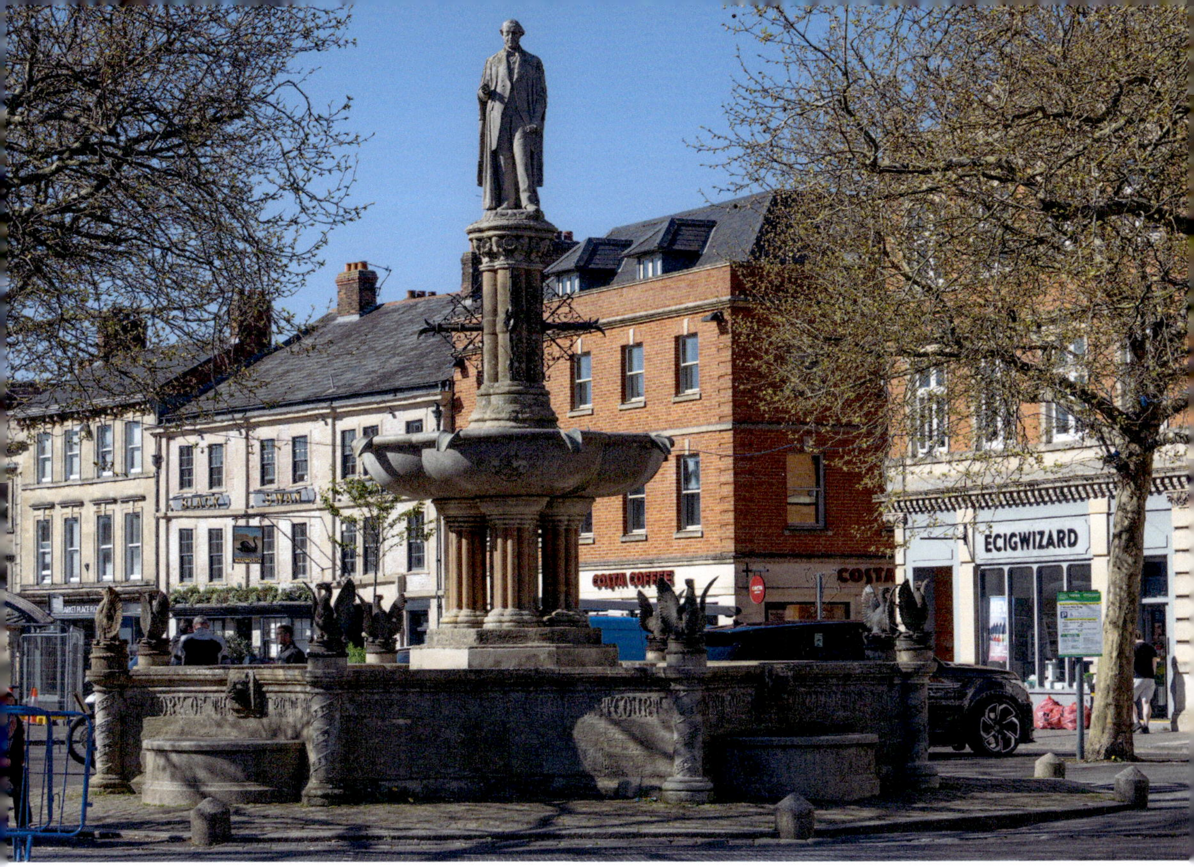

Above: The T. H. Southeron Estcourt memorial fountain on Market Place.

Below left: One of the horse-drinking troughs on the fountain.

Below right: One of the magnificent birds atop a castle tower that decorate the memorial fountain.

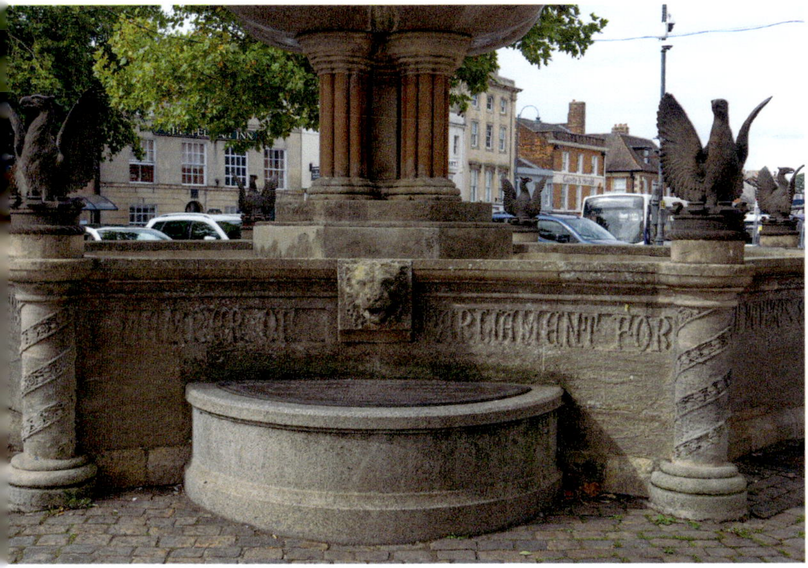

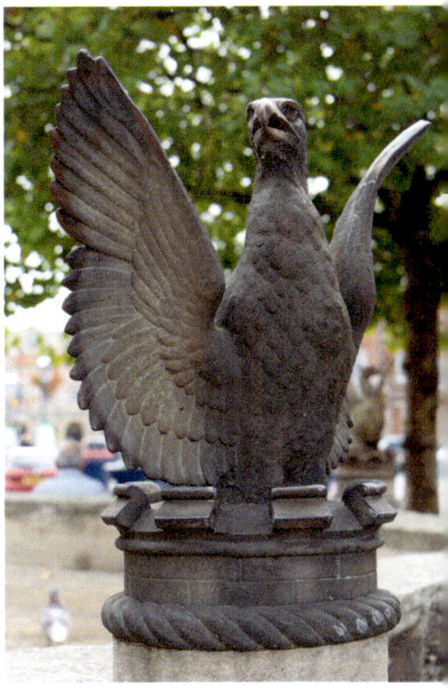

The lower basin is surrounded by seven bronze eagles standing with their wings spread atop bronze turrets at chest height – four in two pairs. The others stand as single figures around the rim of the basin. The sides of the lower basin are engraved with the name of the man himself, Thomas H. S. Southeron Esquire, while the supporting corner pillars of the lower basin are carved with floral decorations. Those who donated to the fountain have their names engraved on the walls of the lower basin.

On completion, the fountain was the first instance of a public water fountain in Devizes. When it was unveiled, the water pressure was found to be far higher than anticipated and sprayed out over the surrounding area, missing the basins completely.

Currently the fountain sits among a small group of trees and forms a group with the Shambles Market Hall and the Market Cross making a splendid centrepiece to the Market Place in Devizes.

The fountain and the supporting structures were listed in April 1954.

Town Hall

Devizes Town Hall stands on St John's Street alongside the building colloquially known as the 'Old Town Hall'. Both were awarded listed building status in 1954. Designed by Thomas Baldwin of Bath, it was built in 1806–08 on the site of the Old Yarn Hall, which dated back to 1575.

While the façade was a completely new design, the new Town Hall incorporated much of the interior of the existing building. The new building was largely financed by local MP Joshua Smith and John Estcourt, opening with a grand ball on 2 November 1808.

In common with its earlier predecessor, the Town Hall is built of warm-coloured Bath stone and stands two storeys high. The ground floor is of a rusticated design with five arched windows facing towards the Market Place. The second floor has five tall windows matching the layout of the lower floor, the centre three with traditional Georgian triangle pediments. Between them stand six Doric columns supporting an entablature and three flag poles flying the Union Jack flag.

Water falling on the roof is channelled away by period lead downpipes, their tops decorated with castings of the Devizes coat of arms below a smiling cherub figure. Once painted in the bright colours of the town's coat of arms, they are now painted a more sympathetic cream colour to match the downpipes and co-ordinate with the warm stone of the building.

Away from the ornate front of the building, the sides and rear follow a similar but plainer style. The side doors remain magnificent in their tall-arched styling flanked by simple renditions of the columns seen on the building's front. Alongside one of the side doors is a brightly polished brass letterbox, surmounted by a brass plaque bearing the simple legend 'Town Mayor'. It is still in use. One wonders if every town mayor is lucky enough to have their own personal letterbox?

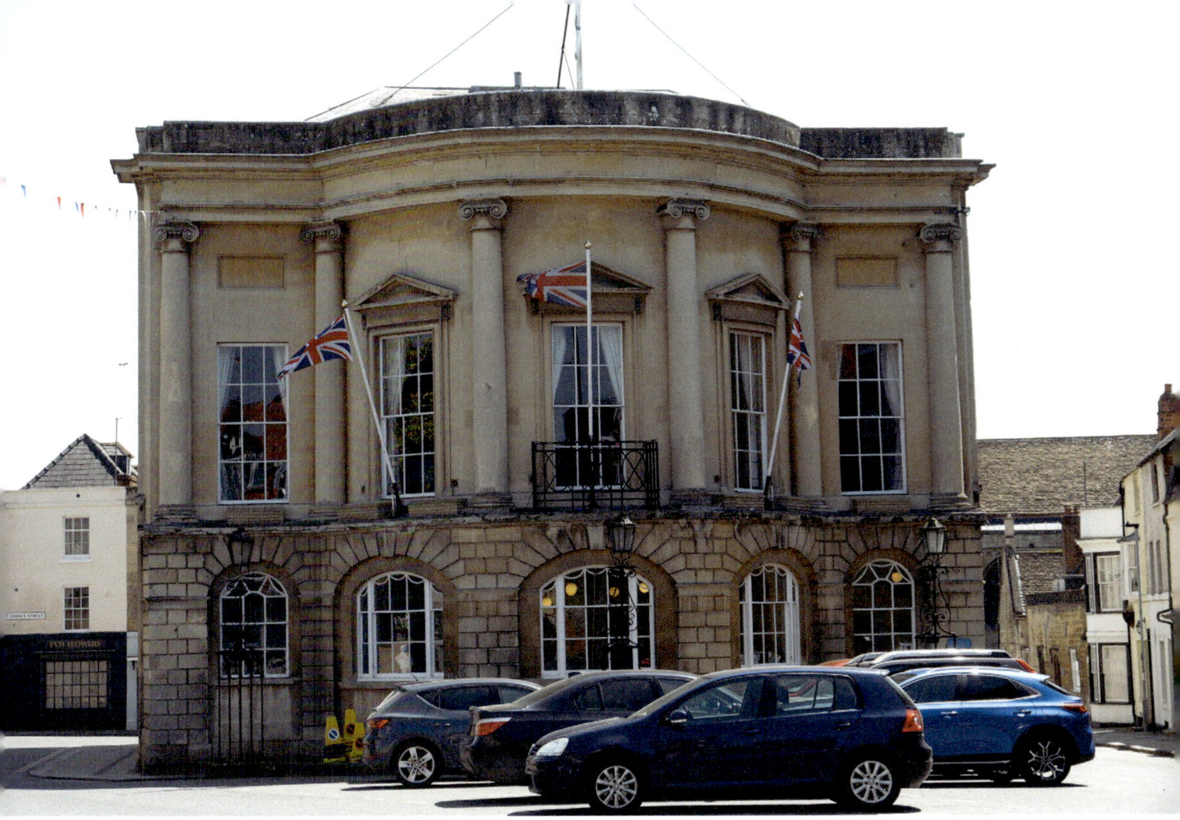

Above: The front of the Town Hall on St John's Street.

Below: The unusual curved rear of the Town Hall with its double-grilled window.

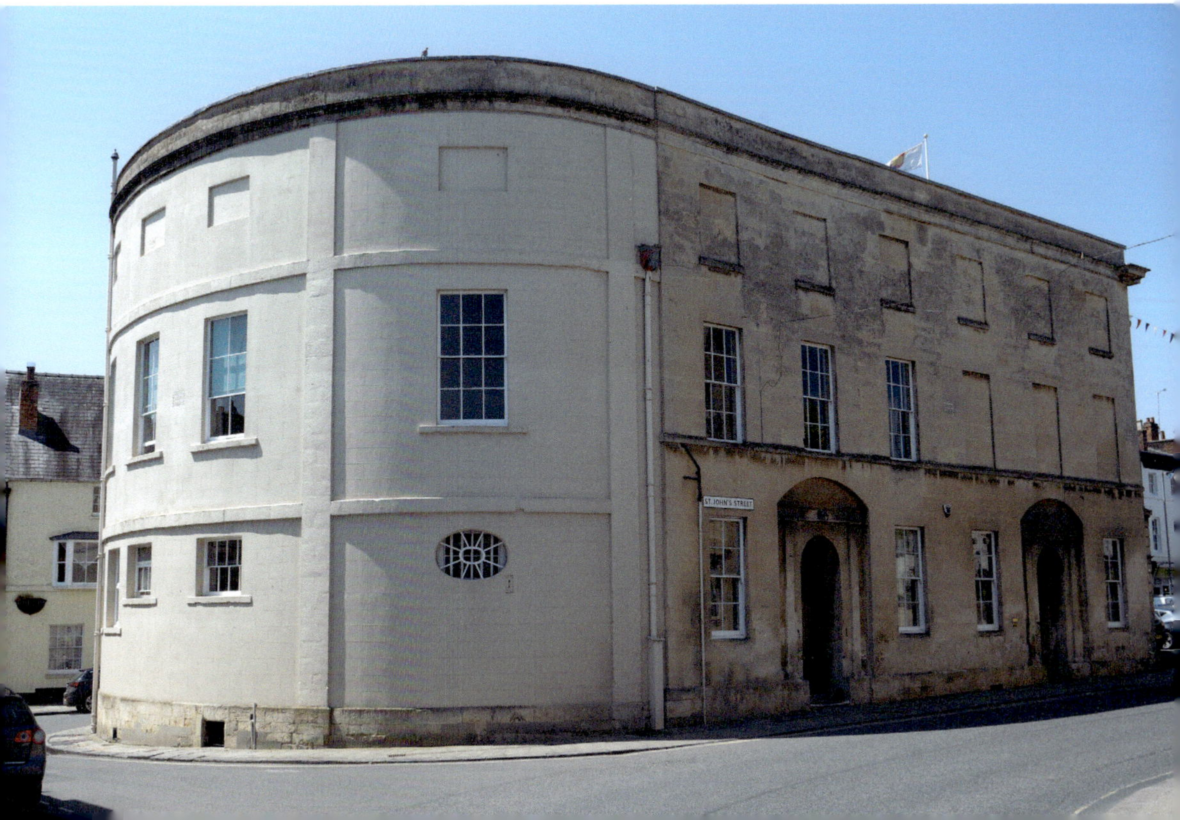

The rear of the building is unusual in that it is curved rather than flat. It sports a pair of oval windows with a distinctive double-metal grille at ground level. Clearly security was as much of an issue at the time of construction as it is as now.

As you would expect of a purpose-built building designed to house the council of a prosperous town, the inside is splendid. You will find a first-floor assembly room decorated with a brightly coloured Adam-style plaster ceiling and a small musicians' gallery above the entrance door – a memory of the days when every function came with the need for live music.

On the ground floor is the Cheese Hall, finished in a range of restful yellows and browns and a wood-block floor. Nearby is a small council chamber, now more regularly used for civil weddings and meetings than council business, but a look at the walls reveals a historical world of framed early documents about the area.

The vaults below the regularly used parts of the building and part of the lock-up were used as air-raid shelters during the Second World War.

Like any building of this kind, the Town Hall has accumulated its fair share of myths and legends, and ghost tours remain a regular feature of the annual events programme.

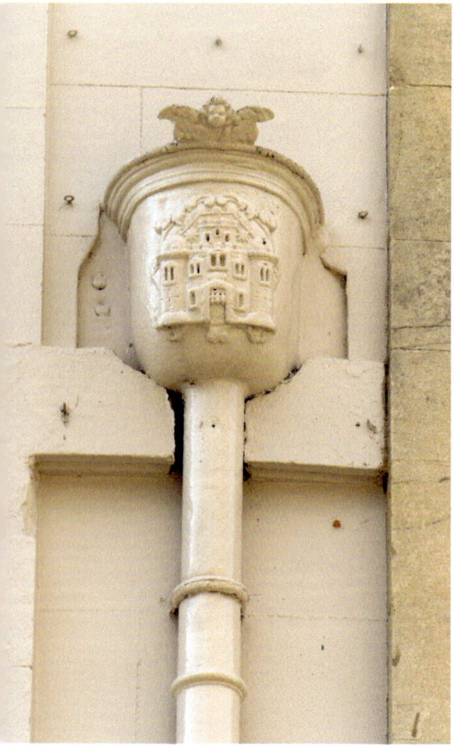

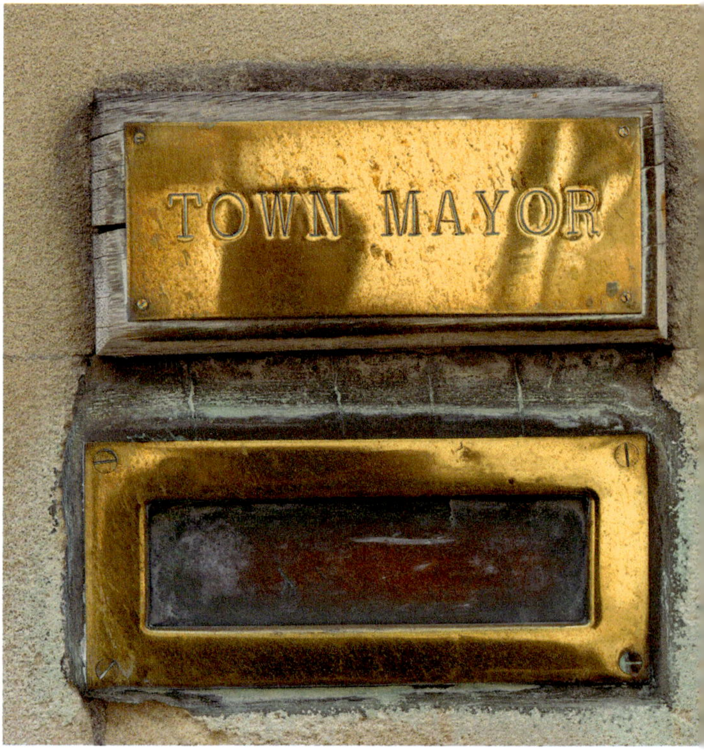

Above left: The Devizes coat of arms is cast into the downpipes of the Town Hall's gutters.

Above right: The special polished-brass letterbox for the Devizes town mayor.

U

Unwanted Books

The village of Roundway stands in the shadow of Roundway Down (see p. 67). It has a tiny village green with parking space for just one car, but it is well used. There is a large and well-kept village noticeboard, a small smartly painted postbox, a rubbish bin and an old-fashioned K6-type BT telephone box. But all is not what it seems.

With the unstoppable advance of personal mobile phones, the public phone here was decommissioned around 2017. Rather than remove the iconic structure, it was taken over by the community and within it they created the Roundway Book Exchange. Locals with read or unwanted books can leave them on the shelves for others to enjoy, while borrowing others for their own enjoyment. When he visited, this author was very happy to note a well-stocked set of shelves and left a couple of his own for others to enjoy.

Roundway village green.

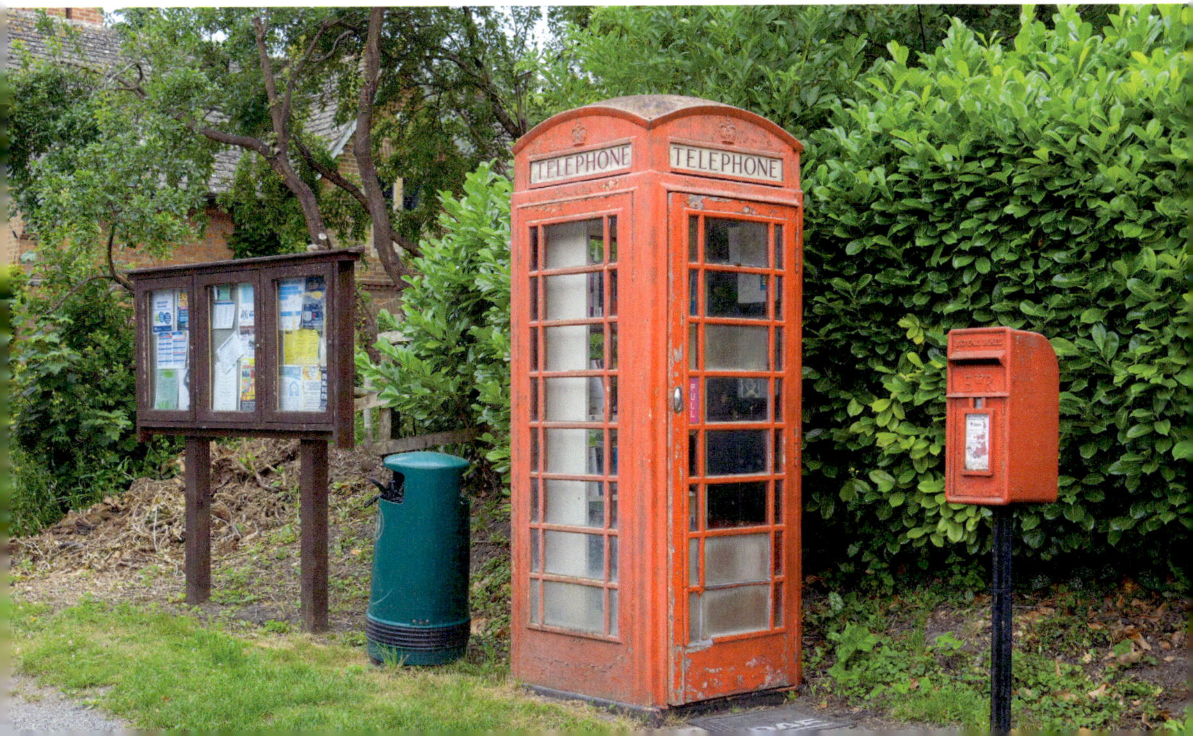

V

Victoria, Queen

The influence of Queen Victoria is still felt in the centre of Devizes. There is a Victoria Road on the outskirts of the town and was once a statue of the monarch outside Kwik-Fit. Most notably, however, is a familiar red object that stands on the corner of Maryport Street: a single-slot, A-type Victorian standard red pillar box, cast by A. Handyside & Co. Ltd of Derby and London. Introduced in 1879, it bears the personal cipher of Queen Victoria.

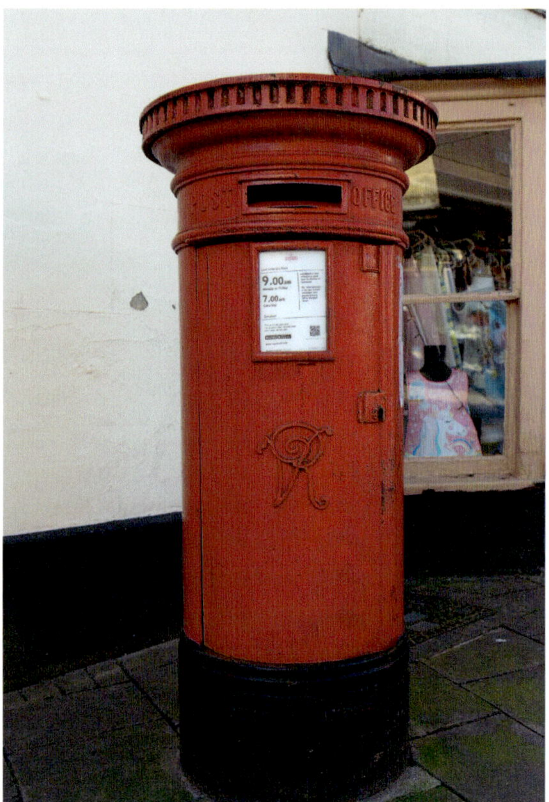

The Queen Victoria postbox on the corner of Maryport Street.

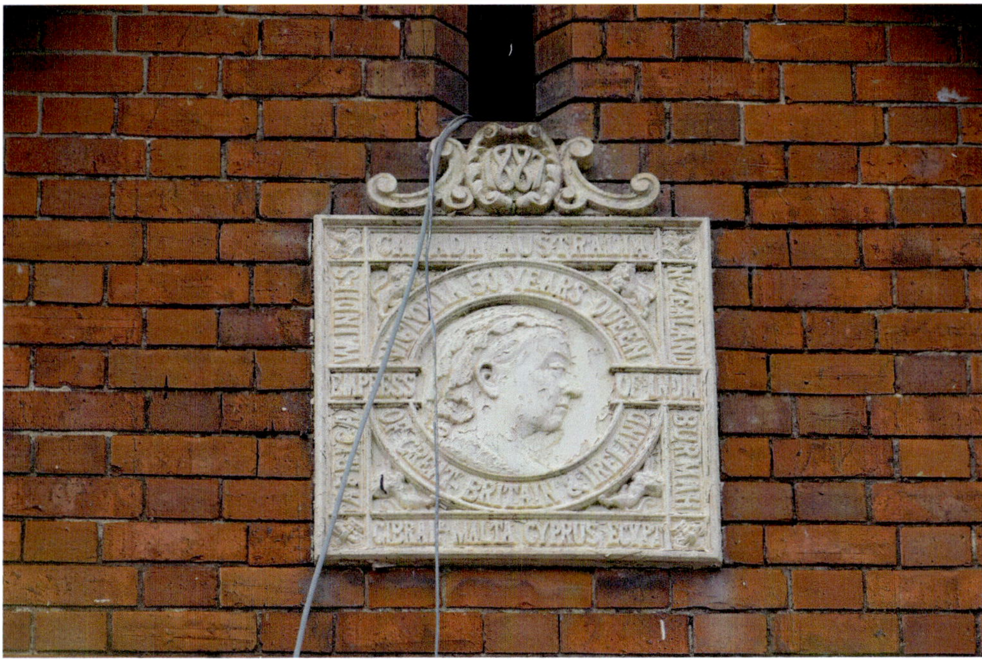

A plaque commemorating the golden jubilee of Queen Victoria on the old Community Hospital.

In a design feature introduced with the hexagonal Penfold-style standard box of 1866 (now you know how Dangermouse's sidekick got his name), the cipher of the reigning monarch was cast into the front panel of every postbox from Queen Victoria onwards. Being made of near-indestructible cast iron, many of the boxes still in use are surprisingly old.

A short distance away, and high on the wall of the sadly disused community hospital on New Park Road, is a plaque celebrating the 1887 golden jubilee of Queen Victoria. Around a profile sculpture of the monarch is a list of many of her titles, including prominently that of Empress of India and the larger territories of the British Empire. Unusually, Burma (now Myanmar) is spelt 'Burmah'.

W

Wadworth Brewery

Standing on the corner of Northgate Street and New Park Street, the huge red-brick presence of the Wadworth brewery is hard, if not completely impossible, to miss. Standing six floors high with an even taller chimney, the company name is picked out in metal letters on the front. The earlier letters spell out 'Wadworth Brewer', while much later illuminated letters spell out 'Wadworth, the quality beer'.

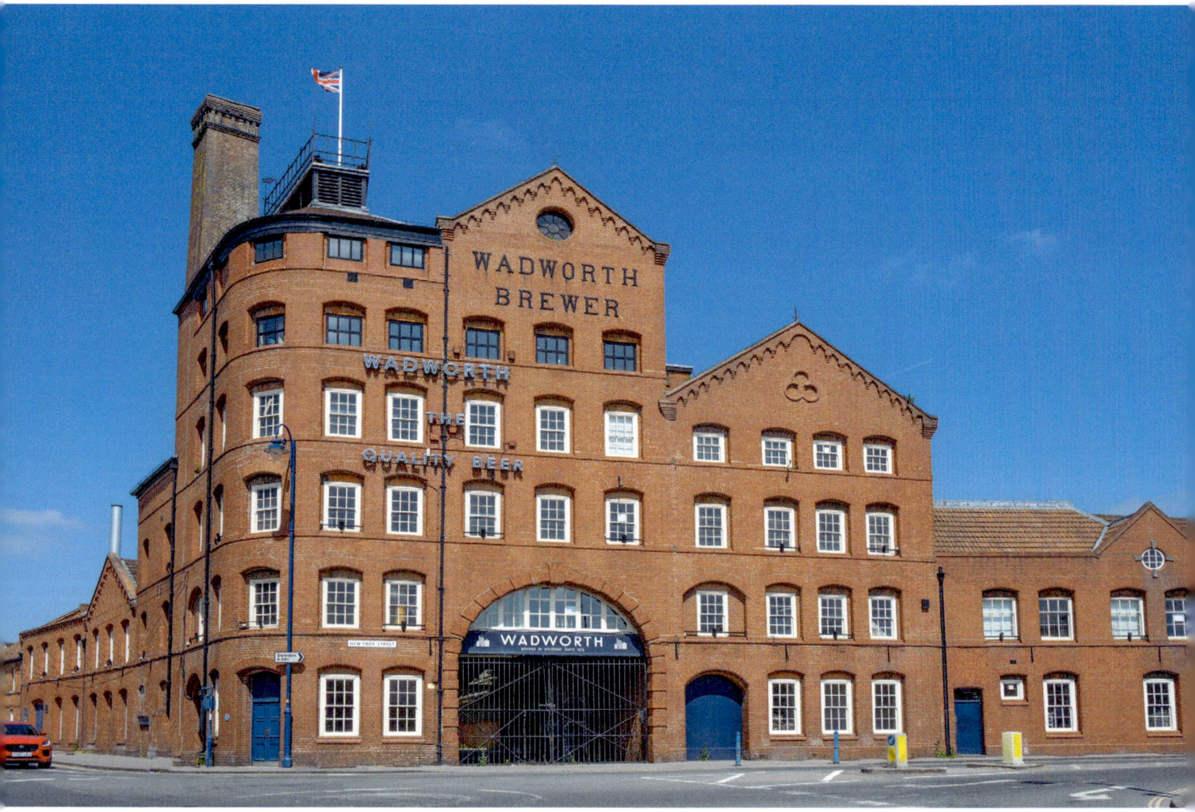

The Wadworth brewery building on Northgate Street.

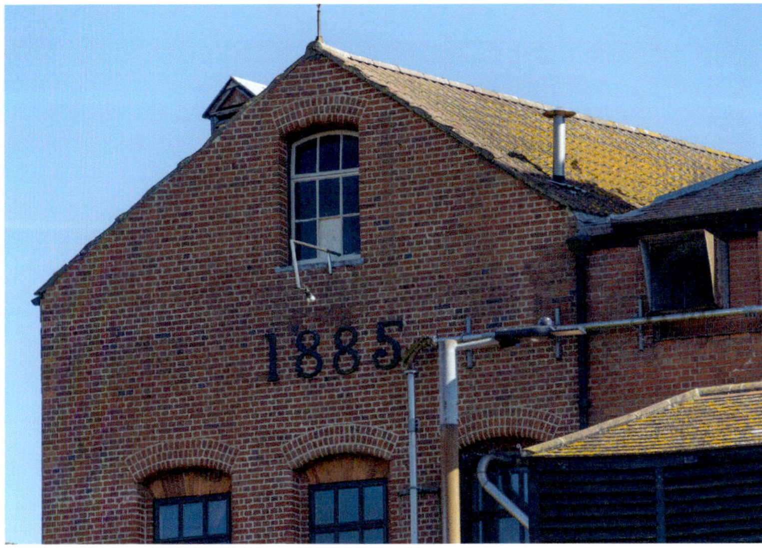

Rear of the Wadworth brewery building, which gives the reconstruction date in tall iron letters.

The building is built so tall so that Wadworth could adopt the tower-brewing method. This process used gravity to move the various brews between stages rather than having to use many expensive and complex pumping machines.

World famous for their beers, the Wadworth's chain of owned and managed pubs runs, at the time of writing, to 140 in the south and south-west of England. Keen to keep up their Victorian traditions and image, every Wadworth pub has an in-house-created, hand-painted and lettered sign.

The front of the building here still clearly displays the original big double gates, made at a time when horse-drawn wagons brought in materials and shipped out the beer. This tradition is continued today; local deliveries are often made by Wadsworth's own team of Shire horses.

Founded in 1875 by Henry Alfred Wadworth, the business was passed to his founding partner John Smith Bartholomew, in whose family the ownership of the business still remains. So popular was the demand for their beers that the production demands outstripped the space available at their original premises. The grand building you see today was constructed in 1885, as commemorated by the large iron letters high on the wall on the rear of the building.

Among the founder's claims to fame is that he was one of the first local men to own a 'bone shaker' penny-farthing-style bicycle, which he travelled on from London to Bath in 1869. A trying journey, one imagines, on a machine with no suspension and solid tyres.

In 2023, much of the actual brewing was moved to a new site on Folly Road in Devizes, but the huge red-brick building still stands as a major landmark in the town. Tours of both sites are available and a must see for any beer enthusiasts visiting the town.

This remarkable building was given listed status in 1972.

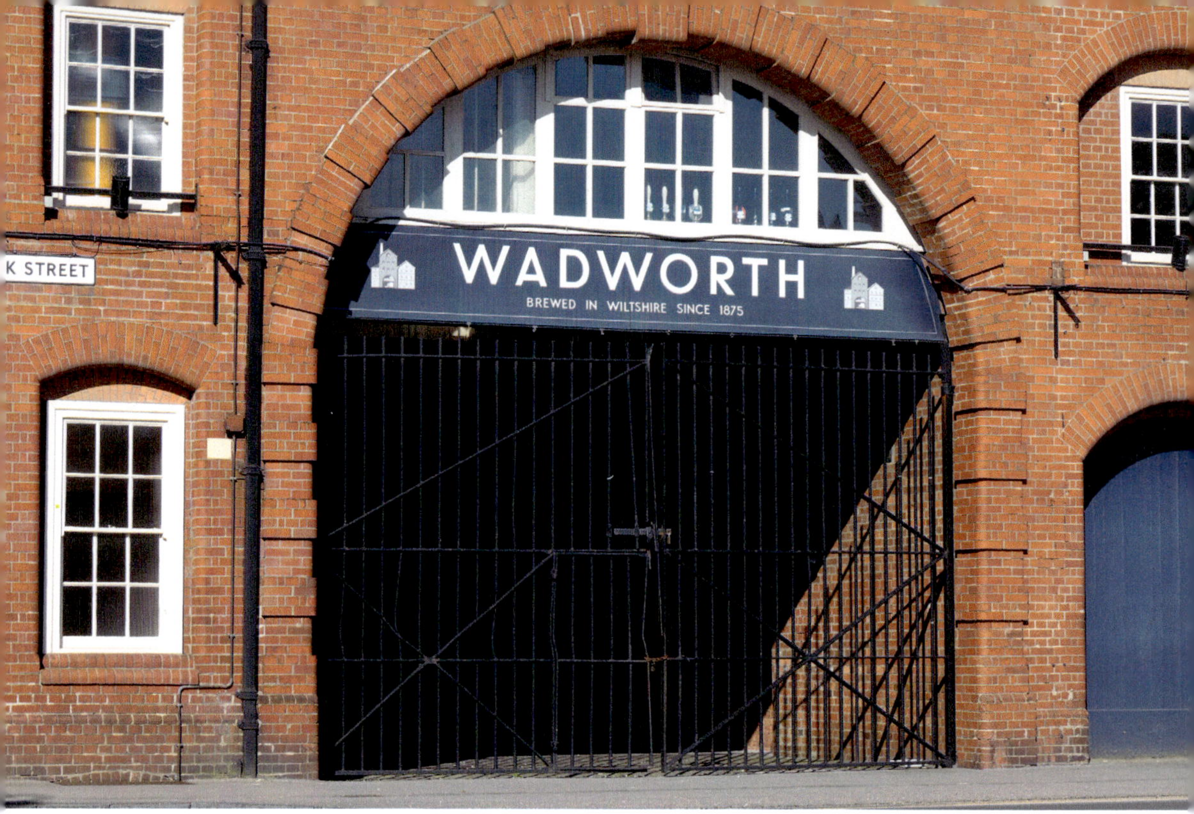

The Park Street entrance was large enough for the horse-drawn transport of the day.

War Memorial

Standing on Long Street alongside St John the Baptist Church is the official Devizes war memorial. An appeal to raise funds to create a lasting memorial to the fallen of the First World War was launched on 2 May 1919. This raised £3,660, which was sufficient to fund the creation of the memorial that stands to this day.

The memorial is a slightly unusual semicircular design of Doulting stone by Francis William Troup bearing six bronze plaques, three either side of a stone archway, surmounted by a bronze urn. Bronze reliefs of laurel wreaths decorate either end of the curved wall, and the poignant word 'Remember' is set into the very top of the arch above the urn in a bold typeface.

The memorial was constructed by Messers Morgan & Sons. The bronze plaques and furniture was cast by Humphy's & Oakes foundry. A small garden of flagstone paving was created around the main memorial surrounded by cast-metal railings.

The large plaques list the names of the men of Devizes and Roundway who fell in combat during the First World War. Smaller plaques list the fallen of the Second World War and later conflicts were added later beneath the originals, the last being dated 2010.

It was unveiled on 13 November 1922 by the Lord Lieutenant of Wiltshire, Viscount Long. The memorial was only given official listed status in 2013.

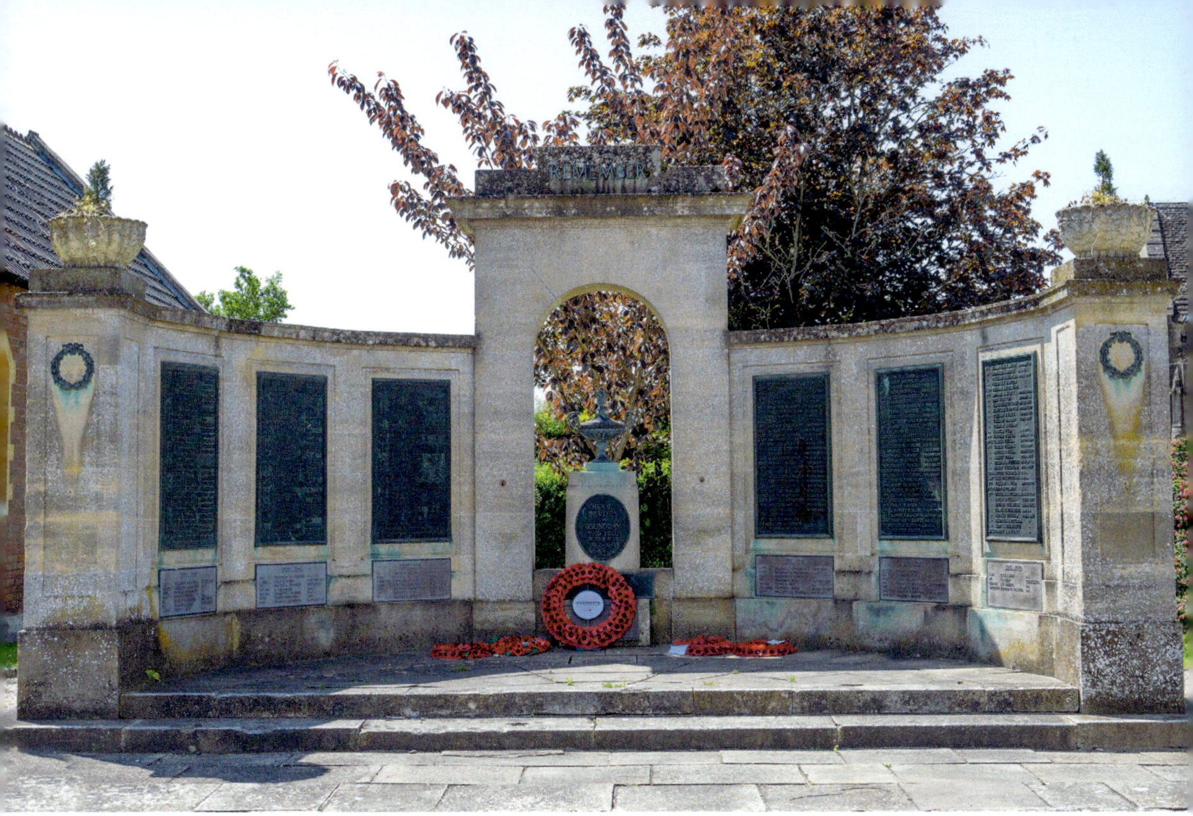

Devizes war memorial.

Wharf

The Wharf is home to the Kennet and Avon Information Centre, Museum and the Wharf Theatre, which was formed in 1947 and remains east Wiltshire's only dedicated theatre. The current wharf in Devizes is the last one remaining of an original seven at this location.

Wharfs are places at docks and canals where cargo is loaded and unloaded from boats for distribution and storage, and where tax or duty is paid on the cargo. Cargo liable for duty were stored in bonded warehouses until this was paid. Both the museum, theatre and museum that currently occupy Devizes Wharf are contained in sturdy buildings that were once such bonded warehouses.

The Devizes Wharf complex was created when the Kennet and Avon Canal arrived in 1810. It is considered to have reached its peak in 1898 when all manner of materials were being shipped along the canal. An 1886 Ordnance Survey map of the Wharf area marked several cranes and a number of gasometers, an old-style circular telescopic building used for the storage of coal gas, as well as the warehouses on the site.

The simple but elegant Cemetery Road Wharf bridge across the canal by the museum is considered a classic of the type, and was given listed status in 1954. Two

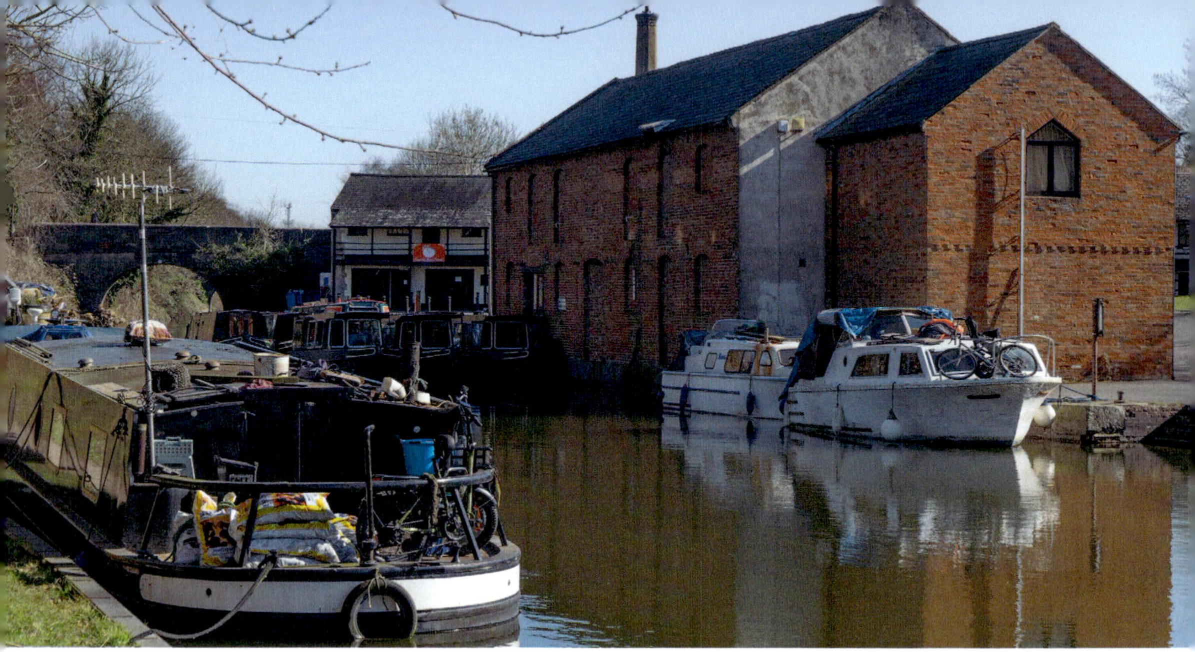

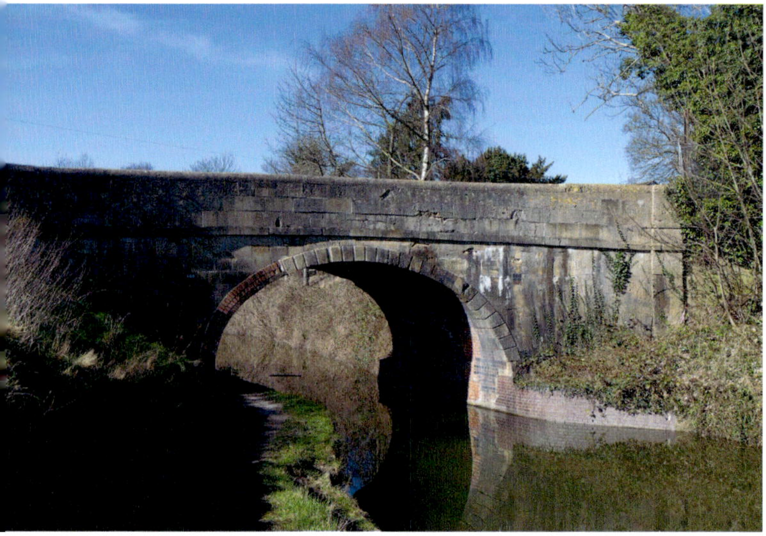

Above: Devizes Wharf.

Left: Cemetery Road bridge at the Wharf.

others adjoin it on the canal, but this one is considered the best and is in by far the best state of repair of the three today.

The most interesting regular cargo handled on the wharf was the active shipping and local storage of large numbers of carboys of acid. The local Great Western Railway was adamant that acid was not safe to be subjected to the motion of carriages on the railway, so it became a major canal cargo. It was stored in the thick-walled warehouses at Devizes Wharf until it was needed for production of fertilisers by local farmers.

During the Second World War, the Kennet and Avon Canal was intended to be used as a stop line should the Germans have invaded. This stop line, technically part of the Blue Line, which followed the Kennet and Avon Canal to Reading, was a line of stationary points or features that would be defended by the armed forces. Opposite

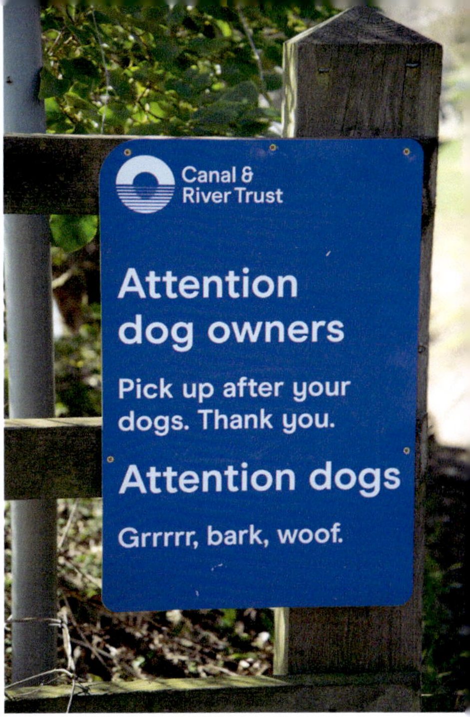

The Canal Trust ensure both parties of dog walkers are well instructed.

the Wharf remains one of the features of this plan: a hexagonal Type 24 pillbox constructed from concrete and hollow bricks by W. E. Chivers of Devizes. Alongside it is a cheery modern sign that exhorts dog owners to clean up after their pets, then repeats the instructions beneath for the dogs themselves to read.

Today the Wharf still serves the canal, though in a rather more recreational fashion. There are moorings for three canal boats with the usual facilities for sanitation, water and rubbish disposal and easy access to nearby Devizes for provisions and recreation.

White Bear Inn

The White Bear Inn (originally known as the Talbot) stands on the corner of Monday Market Street and claims to be the oldest inn in Devizes. Originally a coaching inn on the Bath to London route, it offered accommodation for travellers on a journey that took several days by horse-drawn transport. Accommodation is still offered today, with five rooms available, some reached by a mighty ascent of stairs.

Built in the sixteenth century (the first landlord was recorded in 1567), the timber-framed building with its original beams still visible inside stands two storeys tall with extra rooms in the attic. The front has three gables and a shorter building lacking the magnificent gables is to the left. What the left-hand building lacks in height it more than makes up for through the presence of an immensely tall brick-built chimney added to the property much later.

The original white-stained, pebble-dashed exterior has been retained, and an original moulded wood band is still visible above the ground floor. The right-hand gable has retained its original barge boards and finial, while the others have been replaced, with only their original ornate finials remaining. As with most listed buildings, the original wooden sash-style windows have been retained and painted a suitable period colour.

The front and rear main doors still have their period hood in place with fine oak supporting brackets, while another is far shorter, as was common at the time of construction.

As with so many buildings in Devizes, the White Bear Inn was made a listed building in 1954.

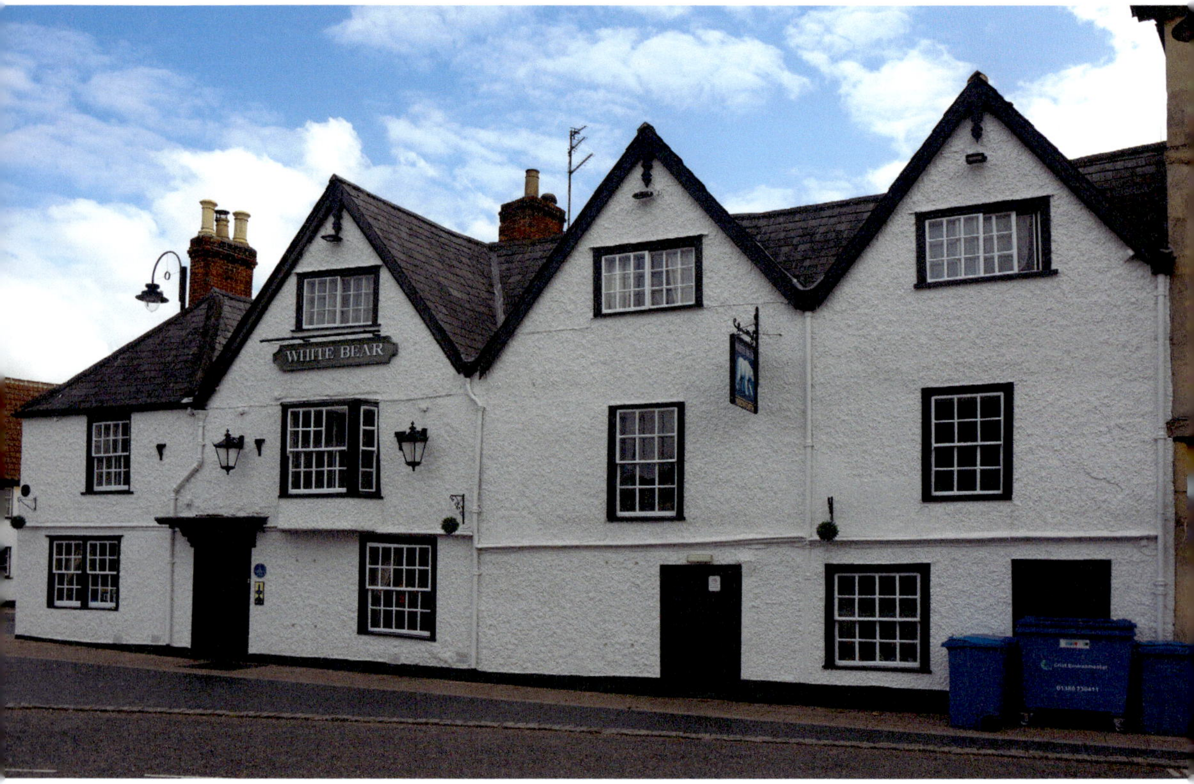

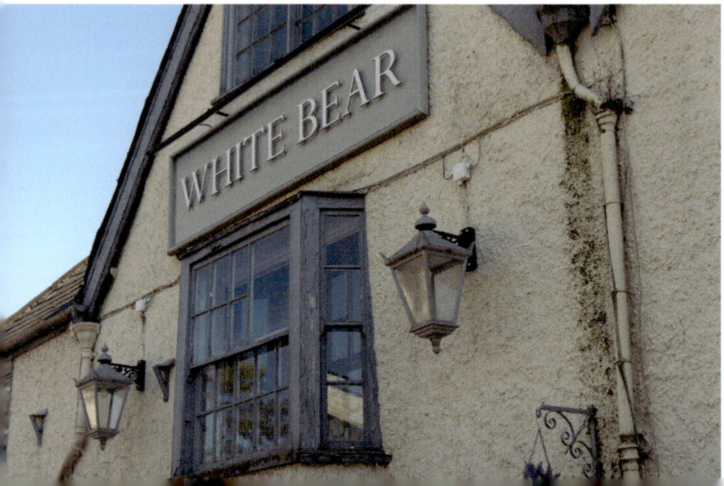

Above: The White Bear public house on Monday Market Street.

Left: Original windows remain on the White Bear public house.

X

X33

If you want to take a tour around some of the beautiful parts of Wiltshire from Devizes and don't want to be shackled to looking out of your car windscreen, you might consider the X33 bus.

Starting out from the Market Place in Devizes outside the unusually named Pelican Inn, you can venture on a scenic tour that will eventually deposit you in Chippenham. On the way you will get the chance to enjoy the delights of the villages of Rowde, Bromham and the town of Calne, travelling along the scenic A342 between. If you are fond of walk, once dropped in Calne head back along the road to the Attwell-Wilson motor museum – it is well worth the effort. Rowde and Bromham, meanwhile, will usually offer you the opportunity of a splendid pub meal if you have the desire.

If you have the urge to travel on even further, the X33 with happily deliver you to the Chippenham railway station (sadly the railways stopped serving Devizes back in April 1966), which offers you onward links all over the UK.

The X33 bus will take you on a scenic trip around local Wiltshire.

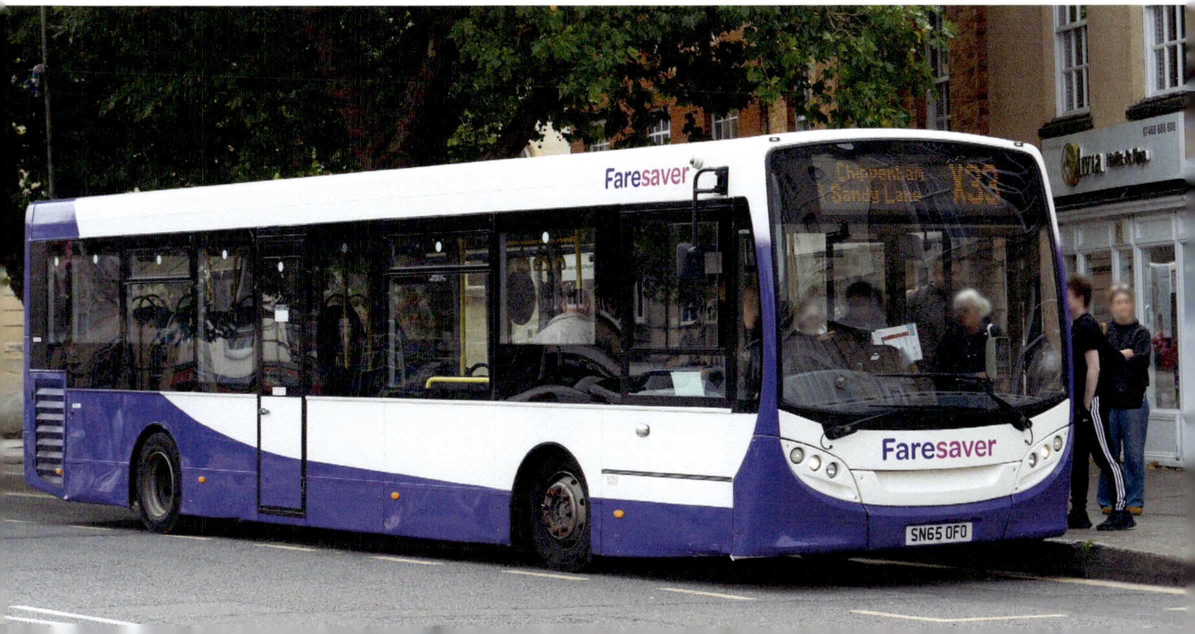

Y

Yeomanry

The yeomanry regiments of the British army started life as volunteer regiments of cavalry, intended to stand alongside volunteer infantry regiments known as the militia.

The Wiltshire Yeomanry Cavalry, becoming the Royal Wiltshire Yeomanry from 1831 (the prefix being given in honour of their service by King William IV, the first yeomanry regiment to receive such a title), was formed on 4 July 1794 when a body of country gentlemen met at the Bear public house in Devizes with the intention of raising ten troops of cavalry. The troops were for the county of Wiltshire in the wake of an impassioned plea in by Pitt the Younger in Parliament for the formation of such regiments in the face of a potential French invasion. Five of the gentlemen present were identified to become captains for the unit. All was made official by the High Sherriff of Wiltshire, Richard Godolphin Long.

After various activities in the service of the civil powers, the regiment escorted the Prince of Wales on a visit to Savernake Forest and would be become the first regiment to be awarded the honorary title 'Prince of Wales own' and to be given the right to use the feathers of the badge of that office on their own badge.

When Queen Victoria created the yeomanry order of precedence in 1884, the Royal Wiltshire Yeomanry was placed at the head of the list of fifty-five regiments – their motto '*Primus in Armis*' is due to the speed with which the people of Devizes responded to the call for the formation of such units.

Despite volunteer units technically not being intended for overseas service, men from the Wiltshire Yeomanry would see service in the Second Boer War (their colours bear the legend 'South Africa 1900–01'), on the Western Front in the First World War as infantry and in North Africa in the Second World War. In late 1941, they were incorporated into the Royal Armoured Corps and converted into a light-armoured unit issued with American Stuart tanks, quickly followed by a mix of M3 Grant and M4 Sherman tanks. Their vehicles were all named after Wiltshire towns, villages and pubs. Following the war, they were disbanded, then reconstituted as a territorial army unit in 1947.

In 1994, on the 200th anniversary of their foundation, the Prince of Wales own Royal Wiltshire Yeomanry was awarded the freedom of Devizes.

Following the many rounds of post-war cuts and amalgamations, the regiment now lives on within the Royal Wessex Yeomanry, providing reserve crews for the Challenger tanks currently operated by three regiments of the British army.

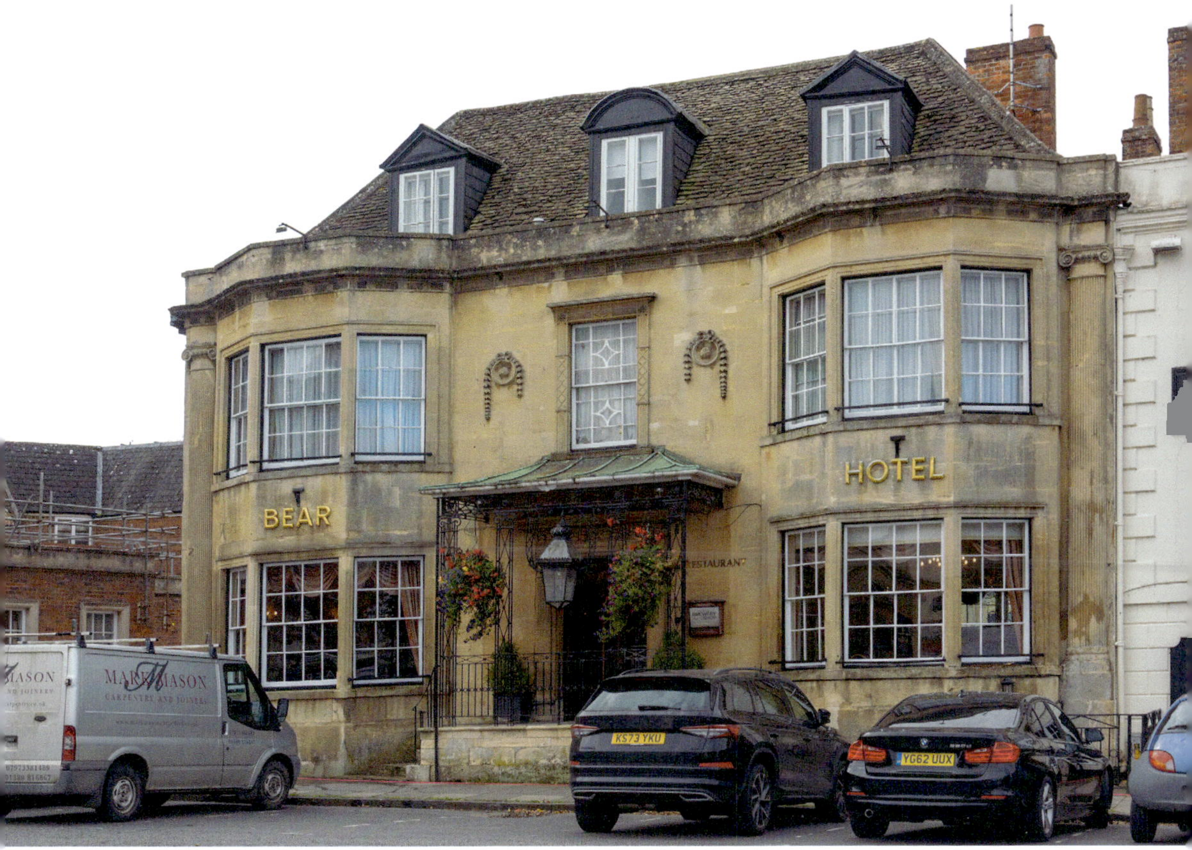

The Bear Hotel, where the Devizes Yeomanry was formed in 1794.

Z

Zephyr Cloth

From as early as the fifteenth century, Devizes was famous for cloth production, the locals often being referred to in reports of the time as weavers and clothiers. They were most notably known for the weaving of Zephyr cloth. This is a soft, white, lightweight, plain, woven, cotton cloth usually used for shirts, blouses and dresses. It is named after Zephyr, the Greek god of the west wind. Today, local involvement in the production of Zephyr cloth is commemorated in a recently built housing development named Zephyr Place.